KORAN, KALASHNIKOV AND LAPTOP

UNIVERSITY OF NOTTINGHAM

WITHDRAWN FROM THE LIBRARY

D0988165

*'the most dangerous moment for a bad government
is that in which it begins to reform'*

Alexis de Toqueville, *L'Ancien Régime et la Révolution*

ANTONIO GIUSTOZZI

Koran, Kalashnikov and Laptop

The Neo-Taliban Insurgency in Afghanistan

University of Nottingham
Hallward Library

HURST & COMPANY, LONDON

First published in the United Kingdom by
HURST Publishers Ltd,
41 Great Russell Street, London, WC1B 3PL
© Antonio Giustozzi, 2007
All rights reserved
Printed in India

The right of Antonio Giustozzi to be
identified as the author of this volume
has been asserted by him in accordance with
the Copyright, Designs and Patents Act, 1988.

A catalogue data record for this volume is available
from the British Library.

ISBNs
978-1-85065-872-6 *casebound*
978-1-85065-873-3 *paperback*

www.hurstpub.co.uk

CONTENTS

v

PREFACE AND ACKNOWLEDGEMENTS

This book is part of a wider research project in which I engaged in 2003, investigating the sources of the crisis of the Afghan state. As the project started taking shape in early 2003, the Neo-Taliban insurgency was just beginning to manifest itself and at that time I was not planning a specific study to deal with it. By 2006, however, the situation had radically changed and the insurgency was manifesting itself in all its virulence in large parts of Afghanistan. It then appeared to me that a study of the crisis of the Afghan state could not avoid looking at its latest manifestation. Quite the contrary, through the interaction with both Afghans and expatriates I felt now a particular urgency in addressing the ongoing insurgency, despite my natural inclination as an historian to wait for social and political processes to reach a 'conclusion' before producing their analysis.

When I started writing about the Neo-Taliban, I initially planned just a 10,000 words article, but it proved impossible to address the complexity of the topic in such a small piece of work. As I was trying to write my article, I felt greatly constrained by the dearth of scholarly literature on the subject and I had to analyse in depth a much larger number of issues than I had initially planned to. The gap in the existing literature sucked me in and compelled me to write something more ambitious than I had originally intended. Little by little the planned article expanded, turning first into a planned series of articles and finally into the present full-size book. That I felt some urgency in writing the book can be seen from the fact that the whole manuscript, from beginning to end, was written in just three months between the end of 2006 and the beginning of 2007, although it was later revised in several instances between February and May 2007.

Inevitably the present volume cannot pretend to be the definitive book on the Neo-Taliban insurgency, if for no other reason that the insurgency was still going on at the time of signing off. However, by early 2007 certain trends were already sufficiently clear to allow some in-depth analysis, particularly with regard to the weaknesses of the Afghan state, which were exploited by the insurgents. This book is not primarily meant to be an addition to the vast 'counter-insurgency' literature, which tries to identify ways to 'resolve' or defeat insurgencies through a purely technical approach, without dealing with the wider social and political context and the characteristics of the state against which the revolt is taking place. This is a book written by a historian who is trying to understand contemporary developments making use not just of the historical method, but also drawing from other disciplines, such as anthropology, political science and geography. As a result, this book combines an analysis of the development of the insurgency based on available information with my ongoing work, focused on identifying the root causes of the weakness of the Afghan state. Some readers might complain about the absence of a more detailed analysis of specific issues which might be related to the spread of the insurgency, such as the shortcomings of the reconstruction/development effort. In this case I answer that on the one hand several other authors have dealt with such shortcomings in a number of publications, while on the other I am not convinced that there is a direct relationship between the insurgency and the slow reconstruction/development effort. Others might complain about the fact that the book does not engage much with the existing theoretical or policy-oriented literature about insurgencies and counter-insurgency. To all these readers I shall respond that in order to produce an in-depth analysis of the Neo-Taliban in time for contributing to the ongoing debate, certain compromises had to be struck. I could have spent (and may still) years reviewing the literature and trying to integrate the theoretical/policy debate more deeply into my analysis, but then the book could not have been published in 2007. I thought that the best possible contribution to the policy debate would have been to produce the first attempt to analyse the insurgency in depth, hoping that some of the policy makers or those who have influence over them would read it. I also hope that this volume will represent an incentive for other scholars to engage with this topic more deeply.

I started studying Afghanistan in the early 1990s, when my focus was the 'counter-insurgency' policies of the pro-Soviet regime in Kabul. At that time already I tried to go beyond a mere analysis of the security sector and deal with the wider political issue of the social base of the state. From 2003 I have been studying the security sector in its interaction with the central and regional elites, the role of non-state armed groups from the 1990s and the jihad movement of the 1980s. All these streams of research, it seems to me, have great potential for enhancing the understanding of the ongoing insurgency and I have drawn from them for this study, as it appears from the footnotes and the bibliographical references. My research is of course still going on, so that this is not likely to be my final word on the subject.

One note on maps: for technical reasons we had to use old maps which show outdated provincial boundaries and do not show at all recently created provinces such as Nuristan, Sar-i Pul, Daikundi and Panjshir.

It would be impossible to thank all those who contributed in one way or another to this book. The present volume incorporates suggestions and advice from Peter Marsden, LTC Raymond Miller and Amalendu Misra, all of whom read earlier versions of the manuscript. I thank them for taking the trouble of going through it. I wish to thank MIPT for having granted permission to use a graph from their website (http://www.tkb.org). Particular thanks to Mina Moshkiri and others at LSE's cartography department, who redrew my maps professionally. James Putzel, director of the Crisis States Research Centre, made available the funding needed for the research, without which the book would not have happened. Niamatullah Ibrahimi, the Kabul-based research officer of the Centre, accompanied me in most of the trips and contributed decisively in making many of the meetings happen. Wendy Foulds, administrator of the Centre, sorted out the logistical and administrative side of the research. Joost van der Zwan, policy & communications officer of the Centre, helped me stay in touch with media and policy circles and also contributed by giving me access to Dutch-language written material. Special thanks go to Vikram Parekh and David Izadifar for their hospitality in Kabul, to Tom Gregg for hospitality in Gardez, to Talatbek Masadykov and Sonja Bachmann for their hospitality in Kandahar and to Valeri Dotin and Mitko Troanski for their help. Several other individuals also deserve to be thanked for sharing ideas and/or advising me (in alphabetical order): Lal Pacha Azmoon, Bernt Glatzer, Abas Kargar, Akbar Kargar, Massoud Kharokhel, Mervyn Patterson, Thomas Ruttig, Abdul Samad, Eckart Schiewek, Michael Semple, Barbara Stapleton, Noor Ullah, Martine van Bijlert and Abdul Rashid Waziri.

ILLUSTRATIONS

Maps

Graphs

LIST OF ILLUSTRATIONS

Tables

GLOSSARY

Al Qaida	a network of Islamist ultra-radical groups, engaged in political violence.
'Alim	Islamic scholar.
AIHRC	Afghan Independent Human Rights Commission
AMF	Afghan Military Forces, the anti-Taliban militias gathered under the Ministry of Defence from the end of 2001.
ANA	Afghan National Army, acronym used to indicate the internationally trained Afghan army (2002–).
ANP	Afghan National Police, acronym used to indicate any Afghan police unit, particularly after 2003.
ANSO	Afghanistan Non-governmental Security Office.
Arbakai	tribal militias in south-eastern Afghanistan.
ASF	Afghan Security Forces, acronym used to indicate militias directly recruited and paid by US forces.
CoP	Chief of Police.
Dawlat-e Enqelabi-ye Islami	'Revolutionary Islamic State', a polity created by a group of Salafis in Nuristan.
DDR	Disarmament, Demobilisation and Reintegration. The standard acronym used to indicate internationally sponsored demobilisation programmes.
Deobandi	Islamic revivalist movement based on strict adherence to Sunna and Shariah.
DIA	Defence Intelligence Agency (Pentagon, United States).

GLOSSARY

Harakat-e Enqelab-i Islami	'Islamic Revolutionary Movement', a jihadi group active in the 1978–92 conflict, from whose ranks came many leaders of the Taliban.
Hizb-i Islami	'Islamic Party', an Islamist group based in Afghanistan and one of the protagonists of the conflict started in 1978.
IED	Improvised Explosive Device (mainly roadside bombs).
ISAF	International Security Assistance Force, a multinational contingent deployed in Afghanistan from 2002 to secure and stabilise the country.
ISI	Inter-Services Intelligence directorate (Pakistan).
Jaish al-Mahdi	'The Mahdi's Army', an international jihadist organisation not to be confused with the Iraqi organisation carrying the same denomination.
Jaish-al Muslimeen	'Army of Muslims', a splinter group of the Movement of the Taliban.
Jamaat-i Islami	'Islamic Society', an Islamist party based in Pakistan.
Jami'at-i Islami	'Islamic Society', an Islamist party based in Afghanistan and one of the protagonists of the conflict started in 1978.
Jamaat-al Ulema	'Society of the Islamic Scholars', a political group based in Pakistan.
Jami'at-i Khudam-ul Koran	'Society of the Servants of the Kuran', a splinter group of the Movement of the Taliban.
Jamaat-ud-Da'awa Al-Salafia Wal Qitaab	'Society of the Salafi movement and of the Book', a Salafi group based in Kunar.
Junbesh-i Milli Islami	a military-political group led by Gen. Dostum and based mainly among the Uzbeks of northern Afghanistan.
Khan	rural notable, normally a large landlord.
Layeha	'Book of rules'.
Majlis al-Shura	'Consultative Council'.

Mawlawi	Islamic religious title.
MoD	Ministry of Defence.
MoI	Ministry of Interior.
NSD	National Security Directorate (Afghanistan's intelligence agency after 2001).
NWFP	North-West Frontier Province, populated by a large majority of Pashtuns.
PRT	Provincial Reconstruction Team, a mix of foreign military personnel (80–150) and civilian elements intended to tie together the military and developmental aspects of security enhancement.
Salafi	followers of a puritanical school of thought based on the example of pious ancestors of the period of early Islam.
Shariah	Islamic religious law.
Shura	'Council'.
Shura-i Nezar	'Coordination Council', a military-political structure created by commander Ahmad Shah Massoud in the early 1980s.
Sunna	the corpus of knowledge of Mohammed's message over which Sunni scholars have reached a consensus.
Rahbari Shura	'Leadership Council' (of the Movement of the Taliban).
Tablighi	Muslim missionary revivalist tendency.
Talib(an)	literally religious student(s), the term is now also largely used to indicate the members of the Movement of the Taliban.
Ulema	pl. of 'alim.
UNAMA	United Nations Assistance Mission to Afghanistan.
UNDSS	United Nations Department of Safety and Security.

INTRODUCTION

'The Taliban is a force in decline.'[1]

'US military estimates suggest there may be only 800 Taliban fighters left.'[2]

'Peaceful elections are a sign that the Taliban are disorganized, weak, and on the run.'[3]

Announcements of an impending victory over the Taliban have been repeated over and over since 2002, particularly after the Presidential elections of 2004, which were said to have been 'a moral and psychological defeat' for the Taliban.[4] In moments of unmitigated triumphalism, some even claimed that 'nation-building' and development work had won over the population,[5] despite much criticism among Afghans and non-Afghans alike regarding the puny results of international aid to Afghanistan and the lack of 'nation-building'.[6] In March 2006, just before the beginning of a series of major clashes, both Afghan and American officials were still saying that 'the Taliban are no longer able to fight large battles'.[7] During 2006 the mood changed significantly and although by the year's end some American, British and Afghan officials were again claiming that the Taliban had been crucially weakened during that year's heavy fighting, the mood in the mass media had turned into one of defeatism and impending doom. In reality, already during 2003–5 a growing body of evidence had gradually become available to cast doubt on the interpretation of the conflict coming from official sources. Rather than being a '2006 surprise', the insurgency had already started developing strong roots inside Afghanistan in 2003 and its spread throughout the southern half of the country took place step by step over four years.

To mark the exact beginning of insurgent activities during 2002 is difficult because after the American attack on the Taliban regime in 2001 the background violence never entirely stopped. Throughout the first seven to eight months of 2002 occasional violent incidents occurred in the mountainous border areas of eastern and south-eastern Afghanistan and in a few instances elsewhere too, such as in the case of a rather mysterious attack on Bagrami district (Kabul) in August. Initially these incidents were attributed to remnants of the Taliban and Al Qaida which had been unable or unwilling to flee to Pakistan and were seen as mainly fighting for survival. In most cases this might have been the correct interpretation—although some re-infiltration also seems to have occurred—however, a spate of terrorist attacks in Kabul and an increase in the pace of guerrilla attacks during the late summer highlighted how something new had started. At that time attacks involved only small numbers of fighters and were focused on Afghan 'collaborationists', mainly police and militias attached to the Ministry of Defence. Attacks against US military installations were limited mainly to ineffective sniping and to the isolated firing of rockets, although some American patrols were occasionally ambushed. The areas affected were largely the provinces of Kunar, Paktia, Paktika and Khost, all characterised by mountainous borders with Pakistan and hence easily penetrable. Only a very few incidents were reported from Kandahar and other southern provinces and some of these may even have been the work of simple outlaws (see Map 1).[8]

Better organised efforts to ignite a large scale insurgency seem to have started in September 2002. A recruitment drive was reported to be going on in Pakistan and Afghanistan, while propaganda pamphlets were being distributed in the villages and the first training bases were being established in Pakistani territory. Throughout the autumn the pace of military activities intensified, despite remaining on the whole quite modest. The resurgent Taliban started planting mines on the roads and rocket or mortar attacks on US bases became more frequent. Helicopters were also sometimes targeted and the first IEDs started appearing on Afghanistan's roads, albeit still only occasionally.[9]

Despite the difficulties of operating during the winter in mountainous areas, the insurgency was gathering sufficient momentum to keep the pace up in the following months and indeed expand its operations. The south recorded the first signs of significant anti-government military activity. Afghan security posts on the Pakistani border of the southern provinces of Kandahar and Helmand were repeatedly attacked, while in Zabul the Taliban were already able to penetrate in greater depth, having found a more welcoming environment (see Chapter 2). As increasingly ambitious targets were selected, the size of the insurgent groups grew correspondingly. In January US forces spotted and attacked an eighty-man unit near Spin Boldak (Kandahar Province), seemingly the largest group of insurgents encountered up to that point.[10]

The build-up in Taliban activity continued during the spring of 2003, when US bases started being attacked with whole salvos of rockets and more sophisticated ambushes on road patrols were being organised in conjunction with IED attacks. Groups of fifty insurgents were now regularly seen in several parts of Afghanistan carrying out attacks, splitting into smaller groups of five to ten men and then fleeing. During the summer of 2003 attacks on Afghan security forces started involving even larger groups of insurgents, often 150–200 strong. In mountainous areas close to the border, like southern and eastern Paktika, it was normal for the Taliban to move around in groups of up to 150. The first Taliban stronghold inside Afghanistan was established in the Dai Chopan district of Zabul, where, according to some sources, as many as a thousand Taliban were based. Although the largest number of attacks was still occurring in the south-east and east, the strongest attacks were taking place in Zabul. During the summer the province fell almost entirely under the control of the Taliban, who were also making substantial inroads in the southern districts of Paktika province (see Chapter 2). Although at this stage the south-west was still lagging behind, in

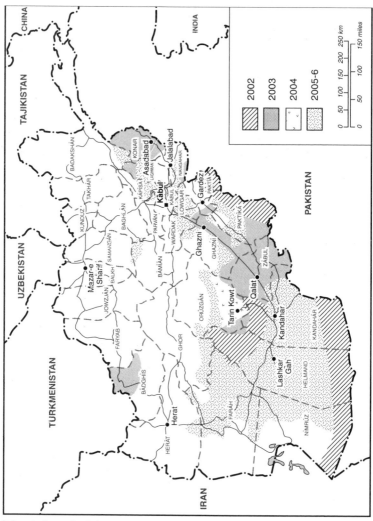

Map 1. Spread of the insurgency, 2002–6.

Note: in 2004 the province of Daikundi was established out of the northern districts of Uruzgan.
Source: press reports; UN sources; AIMS security maps; CENTCOM air operations bulletins.

Kandahar too the presence of the Taliban was growing, with bands of fifty or so active deep into Afghan territory. Throughout Paktika and Zabul they were now moving around during the day and sported satellite phones and new weapons. Even individuals hostile to the Taliban had to admit that much of the population of Zabul was co-operating with them fully.[11]

During 2003 the main achievement of the Taliban was the elimination of government influence in the countryside of Zabul and eastern Paktika. In 2004 they established new strongholds in parts of Uruzgan and Kandahar province. In 2005–6 they infiltrated areas closer to Kandahar city and established strongholds there and in northern Helmand. At the same time they succeeded in virtually eliminating government presence from the countryside of southern Ghazni, much of northern Paktika, some areas of Paktia and Khost and most of southern and central Helmand. Significant Taliban military activities spread to Farah, where districts were being occupied and government officials such as judges murdered. Farah province was easily infiltrated by the Taliban because of its proximity with Helmand, particularly from 2006, once most of Helmand had turned into a stronghold of the insurgents. However, no later than 2005 the Taliban had succeeded in recruiting local commanders in Pur Chaman district, in the mountainous north-eastern part of Farah, despite the presence of only a small minority of Pashtuns there. In 2006 their activities spread to the rest of largely Pashtun eastern Farah (Khak-i Safid, Bala Buluk, Bakwa, Gulistan) and even to the ethnically mixed Farah Rod. Reports by local authorities suggest that at least some local commanders fought on the Taliban's side, while UN sources suggest widespread passive support among the local population. During 2006 the Taliban started infiltrating even Ghor province in central Afghanistan and by early 2007 NATO sources were reporting 'large concentrations' of them there. Infiltration of suspect insurgents in southern Badakhshan was also reported during 2006, with propaganda activity taking place at least in Keran-e Munjan.[12]

In the region of Kabul, which does not share borders with Pakistan, the Taliban did rather well once they had established footholds in the neighbouring provinces. In 2004 they had made their first appearance in Logar and in 2006 they were ready to start escalating their military activities. By that time they had already begun infiltrating the southern district of Kabul province itself, carrying out military activities in Musayi but sending their vanguards towards Sarobi and as close to Kabul as Charasyab. The fact that these areas were once strongholds of Hizb-i Islami might have facilitated the insurgents' infiltration. Towards the end of 2006 NATO had to organise a large-scale sweep operation to clear the area. Although large attacks had occasionally been reported earlier at least in Zabul, during 2006 attacks by as many as three to four hundred Taliban became more common and spread to Helmand and Kandahar. During the battle of Pashmul (Kandahar) NATO estimated that as many as 1,500 Taliban were concentrated in the area. As the end of 2006 approached, NATO sources estimated that the areas affected by the insurgency had more than quadrupled in that year, although this seems to underestimate the spread of the insurgency in 2005 and earlier. The military activities of the insurgents had also increased dramatically. Compared to the previous year, NATO sources reported a six-fold increase in suicide attacks, a three-fold increase in direct fire attacks, a doubling of IED and indirect fire attacks (see also Graph 3).[13]

How and why did this expansion happen? The present work tries to provide an explanation by assessing the sources of the conflict and describing the dynamic of its evolution. The analysis will try to identify which factors were key to the resurgence of the Taliban. The first question to be asked is where the original nucleus of insurgents came from. Chapter 1 describes the 'ideology' of the Taliban and the role of external sponsors. As I argue that the sources of the insurgency are also to be found in the intrinsic weaknesses of the Afghan state, the chapter also looks at its internal fissures, which contributed to breed the rebellion. To fight a war the leadership of an insurgent movement has first to secure renewable sources of recruits, a problem which historically has been difficult to tackle for many rebel groups. Chapter 2 looks at the issue in detail, distinguishing between the original nucleus that decided to start a new war and how that original group developed into something much bigger. The chapter also deals with the different components of the insurgency, which are of great importance in understanding how resilient, amenable to peace negotiations and capable of ultimate victory it might be.

Once an insurgency is underway and starts recruiting successfully, its success is still by no means guaranteed. It needs an appropriately structured organisation to maintain cohesion and to coordinate its activities on the ground. Chapter 3 deals with this aspect and also with the sources of funding which have kept the Neo-Taliban going after 2001. However, even a popular and well organised insurgency might not go very far unless it succeeds in conceiving a winning strategy, pitting its strengths against the enemy's weaknesses. Chapter 4 analyses the strategy of the Taliban in its different aspects: military, psychological and political. Even the strongest strategy will struggle to succeed without at least some tactical proficiency. Chapter 5 addresses the issue, looking at the military technology the insurgents were able to field and at the insurgents' fighting skills.

Finally, no analysis of an insurgency can be complete without a discussion of counter-insurgency efforts, not least because to a large extent they determine the shape of the insurgency itself. Chapter 6 examines the different military actors in the counter-insurgency, as well as the strategies and tactics they adopted. It also looks at the strategies developed by the Afghan government and by international actors to seize political ground from the insurgency and to contain it.

The main argument of this book, as it will emerge from the following chapters, is that despite the role of foreign sponsors, the insurgency would not have succeeded in becoming anything more than a mere annoyance if it had not been able to exploit the intrinsic weaknesses of the Afghan state, both as it was originally conceived and as it was 'rebuilt' from 2001. Without strongholds deep into Afghan territory the leadership of the insurgency would not have been able to spread its influence over much of Afghanistan and would have been left to carry out cross-border raids of little consequence. Strategy, after all, is as much about exploiting an enemy's weaknesses, which the insurgents did. The slow realisation of the sources of the trouble and then the even slower action in addressing these is by contrast the main weakness in the counter-insurgency effort. As of early 2007 the focus was still on finding technical solutions to what is essentially a political problem. The awareness that, as de Tocqueville first pointed out, reforming a 'bad' government creates a particularly dangerous situation is a source of caution. Postponing and delaying reforms, however, is in nobody's interest except in the insurgents' and in that of the Western politicians more concerned with their electoral prospects than with the future of Afghanistan.

NOTES

1 Major General Eric Olson, commander of JCTF 76 in Afghanistan, quoted in Tim McGirk, 'The Taliban on the run', *Time*, 28 March 2005.
2 Scott Baldauf and Ashraf Khan, 'New guns, new drive for Taliban', *Christian Science Monitor*, 26 September 2005.
3 Governor Pathan of Khost province, quoted in Scott Baldauf and Ashraf Khan, 'New guns, new drive for Taliban'.
4 Major General Eric Olson, commander of JCTF 76 in Afghanistan, quoted in Tim McGirk, 'The Taliban on the run'.
5 Tim McGirk, 'The Taliban on the run'.
6 Weinbaum (2004); Rubin (2006).
7 Carlotta Gall, American and Afghan officials quoted in 'Taliban continue to sow fear', *New York Times*, 1 March 2006.
8 '15 killed in attack on Afghan army', *Belfast News Letter*, 8 August 2002; Davis (2002); Jason Burke, 'In the lair of the hunted Taliban', *Observer*, 16 June 2002.
9 Davis (2002); Owais Tohid, 'Taliban regroups – on the road', *Christian Science Monitor*, 27 June 2003; Davis (2003).
10 'Afghan rebels battle US forces', *Reuters*, 28 January 2003.
11 'Montée en puissance de la guérilla des talibans dans le sud-est afghan', *AFP*, 21 September 2003; Françoise Chipaux, 'Les talibans font régner leur loi dans les provinces pachtounes du Sud', *Le Monde*, 7 October 2004.
12 'Un juge afghan abattu dans la province de Farah', *Reuters*, 3 May 2006; 'Over 60 Taliban fighters dead in fierce fighting', *Gulf Times*, 23 June 2005; 'Five Taliban detained in Farah', *Pajhwok Afghan News*, 22 December 2006; Alisa Tang, 'NATO: Taliban set to ramp up attacks', *Associated Press*, 21

February 2007; personal communication with UN official, Kabul, March 2007; interview with Abdul Qadir Emami, MP from Ghor, March 2007.

13 Christian Parenti, 'Taliban rising', *Nation Magazine*, 12 October 2006; personal communication with AREU employee, Kabul, October 2006; Syed Saleem Shahzad, 'Afghanistan's highway to hell', *Asia Times Online*, 25 January 2007; Scott Baldauf, 'Afghan voters face threats', *Christian Science Monitor*, 4 October 2004; Massoud Ansari, 'Almost two years after they were defeated, thousands join the Taliban's new jihad', *Telegraph*, 7 September 2003; Syed Saleem Shahzad, 'Taliban's new commander ready for a fight', *Asia Times Online*, 20 May 2006; 'NATO in Afghanistan', *RFE/RL Afghanistan Report*, vol. 5, no. 20 (1 August 2006); John Cherian, 'Return of Taliban', *Frontline*, vol. 23, no. 13 (1–14 July 2006); McCaffrey (2006); Tom Coghlan, 'British soldier killed by Taliban takes death toll to 20', *Scotsman*, 21 August 2006; Cordesman (2006), p. 5.

1

SOURCES OF THE INSURGENCY

Rumours about attempts by the Taliban to organise an insurgency started circulating in early 2002. Taliban sources at the time confirmed that the leaders of the Movement of the Taliban were in Pakistan trying to reorganise their network and that low rank supporters were regrouping in southern and eastern Afghanistan. However, even members of the Taliban acknowledge that at this stage there was no coordination among the various local groups and no real organisation. Later some members of the Movement would claim that in 2002 a meeting chaired by Mullah Dadullah was held to announce the commencement of hostilities and to distribute tasks and duties to ten top level commanders. The different versions of the beginning of the insurgency agree that the decision to start the insurgency came from a narrow group of Taliban leaders. Why did they do so? Some from within their ranks have stated that in early 2002 they were waiting for some 'offer' from Kabul (presumably for power-sharing), which never came. Hence they were forced to resort to violence.[1] While this might have applied to some of the more moderate figures, who seem to have been working with the Pakistani authorities to put together a viable moderate Taliban party which could then participate in government (see 3.1 *Cohesiveness of the Taliban*), it is doubtful that it ever applied to the whole of the leadership. It is more likely that for 'ideological' reasons they just never accepted defeat and thought it was their duty to fight on. The lull of a few months was probably due to the need to re-adjust, to find secure hideouts, and possibly to recover psychologically from an unexpectedly fast collapse of the regime. Their first attempts to re-mobilise the rank-and-file of the movement were not very successful and few of the 'old Taliban'

11

joined the fight in 2002 (see 2.2 *Early recruitment*). The members of this narrow group of leaders and field commanders were to become the leaders of a much larger movement and they gave to the insurgency its 'ideological' character and defined the direction it was going to take.

1.1 THE 'IDEOLOGY' OF THE TALIBAN

Defining the 'ideology' of the Neo-Taliban is not an easy task, given the lack of transparency of the Movement. However, it can be safely assumed that it is still derived to a large extent from the 'ideology' of the old Taliban. This 'ideology' could be described as a mix of the most conservative village Islam with Deobandi doctrines, with a stress on the importance of ritual and modes of behaviour. Strongly influenced by Deobandi views, the Taliban favoured the reduction of penal and criminal laws to a very narrow interpretation of the Sharia. This was never as evident as in their attitude towards women. Although in principle they were not against women working and studying, their rigidity in enforcing formal dress and gender separation rules effectively led to the complete marginalisation of educated women, at the same time alienating much of the male urban intelligentsia too. Similarly, the Taliban did not favour contacts with the rest of the world, but neither had they objected to them in principle, although from 2000 they became more isolationist in their approach as a result of the influence of their Arab guests. Their rigid application of Shariah just made contacts with the rest of the world difficult and unpractical. Politics, in the realm of the 'old Taliban', was reduced to the demand of an orthodox application of the Shariah, based on a rigid interpretation of the Sunna. As a result, their opposition to the West was based on the rejection of a cultural model, but did not imply a strategic opposition. In this sense, there was no ideology of the Taliban *stricto sensu*, hence the application to the term of quotation marks in this work. It is tempting to see the Taliban as an expression of rural–urban conflict in Afghanistan, but it is important to stress that they were the expression of a specific rural culture, that of village mullahs, and stood in opposition to the tribal codex of Pashtunwali, often ruling against its application (see 2.5 *Taliban, tribes and elders*).[2]

Although much of this applies to the Neo-Taliban too, they also differed from the old Movement on a number of issues. They seem to have absorbed from their foreign jihadist allies a more flexible and less orthodox attitude towards imported technologies and techniques. Not only have they expanded their investment in the production of tapes containing jihadist songs (without musical accompaniment), which they had already been using in the 1990s, but even ventured into the world of video production. A revealing issue is that of the banning of images in any form (television, photography and movies), enforced through to 2001. Already during the years in power the Taliban showed some occasional flexibility in this regard, allowing, for example, foreign journalists to film their fighters (but not the leaders). However, a much more radical departure from the orthodoxy was the large-scale use of documentaries, interviews and footage of speeches in the Neo-Taliban's propaganda VCDs and DVDs, often featuring commanders as well (see 4.7 *Propaganda*). The insurgents carried video cameras with them to the battlefield in order to film the fighting and use the footage for the production of propaganda material. It is telling that at least some Taliban commanders from the ranks of district commander upwards seemed by 2005 to be equipped with laptops even when operating inside Afghanistan, where access to electricity is rare.[3]

More important, the Neo-Taliban became much more integrated in the international jihadist movement after 2001 (see 4.7 *Propaganda*).[4] Their rhetoric featured concepts such as 'global Christian war against Islam' and stressed solidarity with other jihadist movements around the world, which were clearly perceived as part of the same struggle. The internationalisation of the Taliban's 'ideology' might be a key point in the understanding of their strategies (see 4.11 *Mao's epigones, 'Fleas', 'fourth generation' warriors or international jihadists?*), not because of the existence of a serious constituency for pan-Islamism inside Afghanistan, but because it enabled stronger external support. For example, the US-led attack on Iraq in 2003 does not seem to have had a major impact on Afghan opinion and certainly not in the remote rural areas where the Taliban enjoy greater support. However, it is quite possible that it might have contributed to galvanise pan-Islamist sentiment throughout the Muslim world, resulting in greater underground financial support not only for the Iraqi insurgents, but also for the Afghan ones. This, in turn, would have led to the Taliban being increasingly able to fund an expanding insurgency.

One important feature of the 'ideology' of the Taliban was their 'free-market' orientation. There was evidence of this from the beginning of the history of the Movement of the Taliban when in 1994 they accepted financial support from traders to clear up the roads in southern Afghanistan.[5] However, after 2001 they even turned into entrepreneurs. They had no qualms in exploiting the resources of the free market to conduct their war, not only as far as logistics was concerned, but for military operations too. Although the importance of mercenary fighters to the Taliban has probably been overestimated (see 2.2 *Early recruitment*), there is abundant evidence that the Taliban have been paying some fighters by 'piece work', such as carrying out *ad hoc* missions. These could range from firing a rocket at an enemy base to carrying out a targeted assassination (see 4.4 *Establishing structures and a shadow government*). If this reliance on the market was not due mainly to the intervention of foreign services, it would appear to represent an 'original contribution' of the Taliban to the status of the art in 'ideological' insurgency. In the past the free market had been used to run the logistics of rebel movements, such as at least one by the Afghan mujahidin of the 1980s jihad. A number of ideological insurgent movements might have included some recruits motivated by personal gain, but as far as this author knows none ever openly hired fighters for the job.

In any case, the specifics of the 'ideology' of the Neo-Taliban movement matter less than the fact that it had a substantial base of 'true believers'. To all accounts, students of the Deobandi madaras in the NWFP, Afghan village mullahs who had been educated there and the simple villagers who aligned with them were committed and often ready to sacrifice their lives for the cause. US and NATO sources have been claiming heavy Taliban losses since 2002. During 2006 such losses would have more than trebled compared to 2005, to about 3,000 killed. An alternative count suggests that during 2006 about 2,500 insurgents were killed by NATO. The yearly loss rate would therefore be in the range of 12–13 per cent (see 2.1 *How strong are the Taliban?*). Quite possibly NATO estimates of Taliban casualties are overestimated, as was demonstrated in at least a few cases.[6] Whatever the exact numbers, independent sources also indicate that the casualties of the Taliban were heavy indeed, particularly in 2006. A Taliban commander told a journalist in July 2006 that out of eight men who joined the Taliban from his village, three were already dead. What is also evident is their resilience in the face of such heavy losses. In October 2006 NATO sources reported signs of cracking in the Taliban cohesiveness due to the high level of losses, but they had done so at the beginning of 2005 too, citing radio intercepts occasionally showing Taliban commanders complaining about the absence from the battlefield of the leadership. In reality, this interpretation seems to be overstated and despite these losses there was no objective sign by the end of 2006 that the Taliban were cracking. Some friction during an intense conflict is understandable but does not necessarily imply an imminent break-up of the organisation. Those Taliban met by journalists in Pakistan or Afghanistan showed no sign of having lost their determination and faith in final victory, and the reconciliation offers of the government continued to attract little interest among the ranks of the insurgents (see 6.8 *Reconciliation efforts*).[7]

1.2 'REBUILDING' THE AFGHAN STATE: CONTRADICTIONS AND WEAKNESSES

If the beginning of the insurgency was the decision of a small group of men, the choices and activities of another small group of men created a fertile ground for the insurgency to develop. At the end of 2001, as he set out to establish his provisional administration, with the blessing of his American patrons, President Karzai opted to co-opt regional warlords and strongmen into the central government and the subnational administration. The conflict which had started in 1978 had destabilised the provincial environment and created a situation in which the old and well established notable families gradually lost much of their influence as security became the primary concern. This development opened the way to a new generation of 'rougher' local leaders, who were more likely to rely on militias and armed groups to assert their power and influence. At the same time, community affiliations reasserted themselves when the state started collapsing during the 1980s and the centre progressively lost its authority over the periphery. In the southern half of the country people turned to the tribes to provide a modicum of security in the absence of even the traditionally weak central state. Not least because the tribes had lost much of their functionality in many parts of Afghanistan, this in turn favoured the emergence of 'tribal entrepreneurs', who claimed tribal leadership on the basis of a real or alleged unifying role among the different communities in which the tribes had fragmented. In Kandahar, for example, Gul Agha Shirzai had emerged to lead the Barakzais, Mullah Naqib had presented himself as the leader of the Alkozai, Aziz Sarqatib had claimed the leadership of the Ghilzais, Abdul Haleem of the Noorzais, Haji Ahmad of the Achakzais, etc.[8] Temporarily displaced by the Taliban in 1994–2001, most of these figures resurfaced as the regime led by Mullah Omar started collapsing. Of the first group of thirty-two provincial governors appointed in 2002, at least twenty were militia commanders, warlords or strongmen. Smaller militia commanders also populated the ranks of the district governors.[9] In the southern half of the country, the key players were:

- Tribal strongmen Abdul Qadir and his brothers (the Arsalai), allied with Pashai warlord Hazrat Ali in eastern Afghanistan;
- Barakzai strongman Gul Agha Shirzai in Kandahar;

- Popolzai strongman Jan Mohammed in Uruzgan;
- Alizai strongman Sher Mohammed Akhundzada in Helmand.

These, however, were only the tip of the iceberg. In other provinces too and in most districts tens of local strongmen, militia commanders, tribal leaders and local notables who had somehow established a relationship with either Karzai or the Americans were appointed to positions of responsibility, influence and power. This had some important consequences. The most obvious one was that these strongmen were at least in part legitimised through their incorporation in the state structure, despite the fact that for most of them their base of support was quite shaky at best. Another consequence was that the state administration in the provinces was often negatively affected by the need of these strongmen to reward their followers with jobs and positions of influence in order to consolidate their leadership. Strongmen and warlords who became governors and chiefs of police had the legal power to make appointments in the structures they were leading, subject to approval from Kabul. As a result, the provincial administrative departments were soon full of heads of departments who were close associates of the strongmen. The same was true of the local branches of the Ministries of Defence (MoD) and Interior (MoI).[10]

Similar policies adopted with regard to the ministries had deleterious effects on their functionality too. As far as the security of the provinces was concerned, particularly worrying was the case of the Ministry of Interior, which among other functions controlled the police. The need to reform the MoI was recognised at an early stage and a new minister, Taj Mohammed, was appointed in June 2002 with a mandate to undertake sweeping reforms. An elderly man with little support within the ministry, he failed to change anything at the MoI, and in January 2003 yet another minister, Ahmad Jalali, replaced him. He too promised to implement deep reforms, but his achievements during his first year in office were modest. He immediately established human rights offices in each provincial and district police department, and made some efforts to appoint more profes-

17

sionally prepared officers to positions of responsibility, but he never managed to bring the ministry effectively under his control. On paper, he sacked twenty-two out of thirty-two provincial governors and a much larger number of district managers and other officials, but in most cases it was just a matter of shifting them to another province, rather than removing them altogether. Often, when trying to appoint new officials, he faced resistance from the local strongmen, from within his own ministry and from other members of the cabinet. In the early months of his stay in office he sometimes showed a willingness to confront officials reluctant to behave in a disciplined way. For example, in early 2003 he sacked the Gardez chief of police, who was heavily involved in criminal activities. When the latter refused to stand down, Jalali dispatched an armed contingent to accompany the new appointee and even sacked the provincial governor, who had tried to mediate.[11] Despite these undeniable efforts to reassert the central state, towards the end of 2003 and during the first few months of 2004 Jalali's incisiveness appeared to wear off, possibly because he was unable to confront pressures coming from so many sides and to count on the cooperation of the officials of his own ministry. There is plenty of evidence that during 2004 in many cases professionally prepared provincial officials were replaced by unskilled ones, in what could be described as a sort of counter-reform managed by middle-level functionaries of the MoI.[12] Jalali's main political failure was, however, the inability to replace individuals within the ministry itself, which made it difficult to implement any serious policy of new appointments in the provinces. When the time of emergency came and it became essential to strengthen the hand of governors and other administrators in the areas affected by the insurgency, the MoI did not have the capability to do so. As a result Afghanistan's sub-national administration developed after 2001 strong patrimonial traits, looking even less institutionalised than that of the Taliban, of the leftist governments of the 1980s and of the monarchy and republic in the 1960s and 1970s. The system was geared for accommodating strongmen and warlords endowed with their own power base and resources, not for allowing functionaries loyal to the central government to consolidate the influence of Kabul.

In the context of post-2001 Afghanistan, unless they were strongmen governors were not able to exercise strong local leadership even in the rare cases when they might have had the skills for that. The failure of the central government to keep providing sufficient discretionary funds for the governors to interact with elders, clergy and other notables contributed decisively to undermine the administration. If we add that there were few skilled and committed administrators, the consequences in terms of governance become obvious, particularly in the south where state weakness was at its worst. For example, it has been widely recognised that the administration of Helmand was corrupt and ineffective to the point of being effectively 'defunct'. Apart from not delivering much in terms of services, the administration was often behaving arrogantly with the population. The practice of government officials taking goods from the shops and refusing to pay seems, for example, to have been common in Ghazni in 2006. The weakness of the subnational administration contributed to delegitimise the government, paving the way for the insurgency to spread. The autonomous actions of foreign troops, such as house searches and arrests, were not usually communicated to the local authorities, who were thus humiliated and discredited.[13]

The situation was further complicated by the rivalries which crossed the pro-Karzai coalition in southern Afghanistan. A good example of how the effectiveness of this coalition was affected by divisions running within it is provided by the case of Kandahar province. Here the three key players at the end of 2001 were:

- Gul Agha Shirzai, who came out on top initially thanks to American and Pakistani support;
- Mullah Naqibullah, an Alkozai strongman who had supported the Taliban initially and then switched sides in the last days of the regime;
- Ahmad Wali Karzai, the President's brother who rapidly emerged as the leading Popolzai strongman in the province.

This uneasy alliance rested on a precarious equilibrium. In the distribution of the spoils, Gul Agha took control of the administration and customs, Mullah Naqibullah and his associates took the police and much of the MoD-sanctioned militias, while Ahmad Wali initially contented himself with minority shares in the administration and in the militias. The balance of power was bound to shift as the disarmament of the MoD militias got underway, but other changes too contributed to accelerate it. American support for Gul Agha started weakening during 2002, leaving him exposed to the pressure of the two other leading local members of the alliance. Ahmad Wali, able as he was to rely on Kabul's support, was patiently manoeuvring to sideline his rivals and emerge as the expatriates' favourite Kandahari. Mullah Naqibullah, who had long had bad relations with Pakistan and was seen with suspicion by the Americans due to his earlier support for the Taliban, was left without much foreign support and was unable to exploit Gul Agha's decline. In August 2003 Gul Agha was removed from the position of governor and 'promoted' to minister. Although he was able to place a loyalist as governor, this move marked the beginning of a downward trend for his influence in Kandahar. In December 2004 he was reappointed governor of Kandahar for six more months, but never regained the influence he once had, not least because during his absence control of the customs had been transferred to the central government. In March 2005 it was the turn of Mullah Naqibullah to lose control over the police when his deputy Khan Mohammed was removed from the post of chief. Combined with the impact of the disarmament of the MoD militias, this led to the complete marginalisation of Mullah Naqibullah's Alkozais from local power structures. The fight for local control, punctuated by occasional armed clashes between militias and assassinations, ended up with Ahmad Wali Karzai able to control informally local power structures, having 'exiled' rivals to other provinces and replaced them with powerless individuals or with family friends. In the process, however, the old members of the tripartite alliance had been alienated. The departure of the Alkozais from the administration was particularly damaging as they were the main military force within the original alliance and had played an important role in keeping the Taliban away from Kandahar city with their militiamen, many of whom had been incorporated in the police. Only in the context of the rapidly worsening security situation in 2006 had Mullah Naqibullah and Ahmad Wali Karzai renovated their alliance.[14]

The situation in other southern provinces was similar. In Uruzgan, for example, the various strongmen and notables who had supported Karzai's bid to start a movement against the Taliban in late 2001 were rewarded with official positions and then proceeded to face off against each other in a local power struggle, which opened up a space for the Taliban to re-emerge. The most obvious example was Jan Mohammed, a Popolzai personally close to Karzai, who served as governor until early 2006, but the pattern was reproduced at the district level. In Chora district, for example, Haji Dad Mohammed, a Barakzai who had travelled to Uruzgan with Karzai and US Special Forces in 2001, was appointed district governor and was still serving at the end of 2006. Mohammed Gul, a former jihadi fighter who also claimed to have supported Karzai in 2001, was appointed chief of police, but did not get along well with Dad Mohammed and even showed little cooperation with the Dutch after they arrived in 2006. Gul was known as a difficult individual to deal with.[15]

1.3 THE ROLE OF PAKISTAN

The sources of an insurgency are of course not always endogenous, or at least not entirely. Indeed, by 2006 the role of Pakistan in sponsoring the insurgency or at least turning a blind eye to its activities had become a major bone of contention between the Afghan and the Pakistani governments, to the embarrassment of their common ally, the United States. The fact that the Taliban operated from Pakistani territory and used it as a logistical rearguard is no longer controversial, after even the Pakistani authorities admitted to this. However, the issue is whether the Pakistani government was doing enough to prevent or constrain the ability of the insurgents to use

Map 2. Tribes of southern Afghanistan.
Sources: interviews with UN officials and tribal elders, May 2005, January 2006; *Context Analysis Uruzgan Province*, prepared by the Royal Netherlands Embassy in Kabul, Afghanistan, August 2006.

Pakistani territory and to cross the border as they pleased. Afghan frustration at the lack of Pakistani cooperation was shared by some NATO countries, which were by then directly exposed to Taliban attacks in southern Afghanistan. A NATO mission to Pakistan in November 2006 tried to enlist a greater Pakistani cooperation, as did US Secretary of State Condoleeza Rice during her visit to Islamabad at the beginning of the summer. Before that, countless meetings involving the leaderships of either or both the two countries and often US representatives too, including, once, President Bush himself, had taken place in Islamabad, Kabul, Washington and elsewhere.[16]

However, all these efforts achieved the same result, that is very little. In January 2002 the Pakistani authorities arrested some Taliban figures, such as Ambassador to Pakistan Mullah Zaif and a few others, none of whom was known as a military commander or had played a key role in the regime. Again at the end of the summer of 2004 some former Taliban were arrested, including former Deputy Foreign Minister Mullah Jalil, allegedly a close ally of Mullah Omar. In 2005 a new apparent crackdown yielded the capture of Abdul Latif Hakimi, spokesman of the Taliban. However, up to 2006 Pakistan had on the whole arrested just a handful of Taliban, compared to about a thousand 'Al Qaida' activists. As international pressure increased during 2006, the Pakistani authorities tried to appease their Afghan counterparts and NATO with a more substantial gesture, at least in appearance. They rounded up and deported to Afghanistan large numbers of alleged Taliban. The arrests started in July 2006, shortly after Condoleeza Rice's visit to Pakistan. A new wave of arrests took place in November 2006, in correspondence with renewed international pressure. In total 500 alleged Taliban were arrested in Pakistan in 2006, of which about 400 were handed over to Afghanistan. However, the Afghan authorities finally had to release the deportees as they did not appear to be involved with the Taliban, or at least the Pakistani authorities failed to provide any evidence of such. The 'suspects' were handed over to the Afghan authorities apparently on the basis that they could not speak Urdu and were unaware of their whereabouts, although some had been arrested during a raid against a madrasa. In January 2007 another crackdown was announced in Baluchistan, with the arrest of 400 'Taliban suspects'. Only in February 2007 were there signs that Pakistan might finally be beginning to place the leadership of the Taliban under serious pressure, following US Vice-President Cheney's visit and possibly the delivery of precise information concerning the whereabouts of key Taliban commander Mullah Obeidullah, who was then arrested barely hours after Cheney's departure. However, there were strong allegations that another important leader of the insurgency was captured with Obeidullah and then freed, which if true would point to a still less than total commitment of Pakistan in suffocating the insurgency.[17]

In addition to their doubtful cooperation against the Taliban, the Pakistani authorities started to retaliate against Afghan accusations of complicity in the insurgency. In November 2006 they accused the Afghan National Security Directorate (NSD) of involvement in terrorist attacks in the Pakistani NWFP. According to the Pakistanis, a number of Afghan Uzbeks connected with the NSD were arrested after the attacks and a few were even reported to have admitted their contacts with the Afghan intelligence.[18]

The exact role of the Pakistani government in the insurgency is not easy to pin down. Some Pakistani experts believe that some elements in the military and intelligence establishment misled President General Musharraf on Afghanistan and misrepresented the situation. The interpretation that Pakistani agencies might not be acting in a unified way is lent some credibility by the fact that this had already occurred in the 1990s when the victim had been Benazir Bhutto,[19] and is also confirmed by ISAF sources which reported how in some instances the Pakistani army and air force cooperated with US and NATO forces in fighting against cross-border raids. On the other hand, there is evidence that the Pakistan ISI protected Taliban leaders and bases in and around Quetta, including by keeping away journalists and other unwanted presences, and that Pakistani border guards allowed the insurgents to freely cross the border in their presence. A high-ranking Pakistani official, Lt Gen. Safdar Hussein, who was in charge of operations in the NWFP, admitted that the insurgents were operating from Pakistan as early as 27 July 2005. In February 2007 even President Musharraf was forced to admit that in some cases Pakistani border forces had turned a 'blind eye' to the militants crossing the border. Many observers believe that elements within the ISI or former members of that service do help the Taliban directly and some claim to have seen evidence of it.[20] Some observers within the US government even believe the ISI is still providing intelligence and tactical information to the Taliban.[21] Certainly, some former operatives of the ISI and former Pakistani army officers do not hide their strong sympathy for them. There is also some evidence of retired ISI or army officers travelling to locations under Taliban control in Afghanistan to meet leaders of the insurgency. However, evidence is lacking with regard to direct supplies of weapons to the rebels. Some considerations tend to confirm that the Taliban have been receiving some advice from external sources. The main one among them is the adoption of a relatively sophisticated strategy—inspired in part by Mao's theories and in part by the Iraqi experience—by a Taliban leadership which was never known for being well read or sophisticated (see Chapter 4). This would not exclude Arab militants from the potential 'advisors' who could have helped the Taliban develop their strategy and they must certainly have played a role with regard to certain aspects, such as bomb attacks. However, the much stronger stress on traditional guerrilla tactics compared to Iraq and the skills with which the Taliban have targeted different sections of Afghan society suggest the presence of 'cooler' heads and of advisors with long-standing experience of Afghanistan, such as current or former ISI operatives. [22]

If the Taliban receive advice and intelligence from sources like the ISI, this does not imply that they receive hardware from the same sources. Although Gen. Jones of the US Armed Forces stated to the US Senate in September 2006 that the ISI provides aid to the Taliban Shura of Quetta, there is in fact little available evidence that the rebels receive large amounts of weaponry from any single source. Clearly weapons were being purchased on the black market and from several different sources:

- Afghan officials themselves admitted that many of the Taliban's weapons come from or through northern Afghanistan, where they are purchased on the black market;
- in February 2006 a Toyota loaded with weapons was intercepted by the Afghan police on a highway in Baghlan;

- in August 2006 several MoD officers were arrested in Chara-siab for trafficking weapons and ammunition to the Taliban in Logar;
- police sources also confirmed that during Taliban offensives in the south, arms prices peaked in northern Afghanistan: over the summer of 2006 the price of weapons doubled in northern Afghanistan, in part because local commanders were also beginning to rearm; by early 2007 prices of Kalashnikovs were four times as high as in early 2004;
- even greater increases were recorded in the arms markets of the Pakistan North-west Frontier Province, where the price of bullets increased as much as twenty-fold. Hence, if the ISI or the Pakistani army supply the Taliban, they clearly do not give enough to satisfy their requirements fully;
- the involvement of international NGO staff in arms trafficking was also highlighted by the arrest of two foreign nationals in Kabul in December 2006;
- illegal imports of weapons destined to the insurgency are also reported from Iraq via Iran, according to police sources;
- Taliban sources and widespread rumours alleged that ammunition deliveries to the Ghorak district of Kandahar were regularly ending up in the hands of the Taliban, as well as in other districts where administrators traded their supplies for immunity from Taliban attacks.[23]

Whatever the actual role of the Pakistani state in the conflict, the simple fact that most Afghans believe that it is behind the Taliban was a major factor in the conflict. In some cases this played against the Taliban, as the Pashtunistan issue remains alive and well in the consciousness and political culture of Afghan Pashtuns, who often claim the Pashtun lands of Pakistan for the Afghan state. This was particularly the case of the south-east and of Nangarhar province, where Pashtun/Afghan nationalism has deeper roots than in other parts of the country. However, in most other cases the contrary was true and the Taliban might well have benefited from their alleged association with Pakistan. In this sense Kabul's anti-Pakistan propaganda might have been counter-productive. Pakistani influence in southern Afghanistan is paramount, with most economic activity and trade taking place in Pakistani Rupees. The tribes living across the border tend to be attracted more strongly towards the Pakistani side because that is where the economic weight is, while inter-marriage tends to consolidate this influence. In this context, the inability of the Americans to bring sufficient pressure to bear on the Pakistan government to force it to stop the insurgents' activities might have resulted in a belief among Afghans that being on the pro-Pakistan side in the conflict was wiser, as Pakistan was going to be involved in Afghanistan much longer and more effectively than the United States.[24]

However, in a sense the influence of Pakistan in Afghanistan is also a case of attraction exercised by the NWFP, possibly even more than by Pakistan as such. Although the economics of influence worked in favour of Pakistan in the short term, the underlying sentiment might not necessarily be so sympathetic to Pakistan. At least some members of the Taliban seem to have resented the pressure of Pakistani security services, accusing them of forcing the Taliban to attack schools and development projects to prevent Afghanistan from progressing as a country. In this regard there are some indications that the Pakistani authorities might be worried about the simultaneous development of strong Taliban movements in both Afghanistan and the NWFP. Given the obviously strong connection between the two movements, the prospect of a politically unified 'Pashtunistan in being' must be alarming for the Pakistanis, even if that had to happen under an Islamic banner. Some sources allege that the ISI was developing contacts and supporting non-Taliban and non-Hizb insurgent groups in southern and south-eastern Afghanistan, as well as particular individuals and groups within the Afghan Taliban Movement who were seen as more amenable to Pakistani influence and direction. Such sources point out how mainstream Taliban distance themselves from a number of commanders and representatives who are known to be very close to the Pakistanis and rumoured to receive instructions directly from them. If this is true, the insistence of the Pakistani leadership on the need for the Afghan government to negotiate with the Taliban, reiterated several times during 2006, would be easier to understand. In order to prevent the Talibanisation of the two halves of Pashtunistan from continuing and converging, the Pakistanis needed a political deal to set in stone the influence gained so far inside Afghanistan and to freeze the process of radicalisation going on at the grassroots level.[25]

1.4 THE ROLE OF IRAN

There is plenty of evidence that the Islamic Republic of Iran has been actively trying to expand and consolidate its influence in Afghanistan and is carrying out propaganda activities against the US presence. In November 2006 Iranian President Ahmadinejad even stated openly on state television that the foreign troops 'occupying' Afghanistan should leave. However, there is little evidence to substantiate allegations that Teheran has been supporting the Taliban or other insurgent groups. Part of the Afghan press repeatedly published reports concerning alleged Iranian support for insurgent groups in Afghanistan, echoing claims by local administration officials and police officers in western Afghanistan. Some Afghans confirmed such claims to Western journalists, citing anecdotal evidence of direct supplies of weapons and of wounded Taliban being treated in Iran. Some Iranian weapons were found in Panjwai and elsewhere, but Taliban sources claimed to have been purchasing weapons from Iran and not to have received them for free. The fact that the weapons (mortar shells and plastic explosive) were marked as manufactured in Iran militates against Teheran's involvement, as it would likely have been more careful. Even US sources acknowledge that there is no proof of shipments of arms from Iran state agencies to non-state armed groups in Afghanistan. In sum, it does not appear that the Iranians by early 2007 had gone farther than establishing contacts with groups involved in the insurgency, possibly aiming to identify potential targets to retaliate against in the event of American military intervention in Iran. Transfer of cash to leaders of non-state groups seems to have occurred, but the insurgents do not seem to have figured among them. Some diplomats even believe that preventing the Taliban from regaining power in Afghanistan remains a priority for Teheran. In fact, due to Afghan-Pakistani tensions, Iran had already plenty of leverage to influence its eastern neighbour, which increasingly relied on Iran for its trade. Claims that Iran supported Hizb-i Islami after 2002 are similarly unsupported. Gulbuddin Hekmatyar, the leader of Hizb-i Islami, resided in Iran until February 2002. Following the closure of the offices of his party and threats to deport him if he did not water down his militant rhetoric, the Iranian authorities asked him to leave the country. While it is certainly possible that Hekmatyar might have maintained contacts with the Iranians after he left the country, his presumed location in eastern Afghanistan would clearly prevent large scale Iranian support. Moreover, there was no sign up to 2006 of a major effort to revitalise Hekmatyar's following in western Afghanistan.[26]

NOTES

1   Zahid Hussain, 'Taliban's chiefs keep in trim for comeback', *The Times*, 29 March 2002; Owais Tohid, 'Taliban regroups – on the road', *Christian Science Monitor*, 27 June 2003; Elizabeth Rubin, 'In the land of the Taliban', *New York Times Magazine*, 22 October 2006.
2   Maley (1998), p. 15; Dorronsoro (2005), pp. 299-301, 310–11; Rashid (1999); Roy (1998), pp. 210–11.
3   Baily (2001), p. 37; Syed Saleem Shahzad, 'How the Taliban prepare for battle', *Asia Times Online*, 5 December 2006; Dixit (n.d.); Hamid Mir, 'The Taliban's new face', *Rediff* (India), 27 September 2005.
4   See also the interview with a pro-Taliban Mawlawi in Nivat (2006), pp. 89–91.
5   See Rashid (2000), pp. 22, 190–1.
6   See for example 'Taliban death toll inaccurate', *BBC News*, 10 December 2006.
7   '2,000 militants killed in special forces operations in Afghanistan since Sept. 1', *Associated Press*, 13 December 2006; Jason Burke, 'Hunt for the Taliban trio intent on destruction', *Observer*, 9 July 2006; Tom Coghlan, 'Taliban

train snipers on British forces', *Daily Telegraph*, 23 July 2006; personal communication with high-ranking British officer, Kabul, October 2006; Tim McGirk, 'The Taliban on the run', *Time*, 28 March 2005.

8   Interview with Ustad Abdul Haleem, Kandahar, January 2006.

9   Assessment carried out during fieldwork in Afghanistan.

10 See Giustozzi (2004) for more details.

11 International Crisis Group (2003b), p. 5; interview with Jalali in *PakTribune*, 12 April 2004.

12 Interviews with UN officials in Kunduz, Kabul, Mazar and Herat, October 2003–April 2004.

13 Interview with Massoud Kharokhel, 1 October 2006, Tribal Liaison Office, Kabul; Declan Walsh and Bagarzai Saidan, 'Across the border from Britain's troops, Taliban rises again', *Guardian*, 27 May 2006; Sara Daniel, 'Afghanistan: "Résister aux talibans? A quoi bon!"', *Le Nouvel Observateur*, 10 August 2006. For the opinion of US Ambassador Neumann on the impact of a weak administration see David Rohde and James Risen, 'C.I.A. review highlights Afghan leader's woes', *New York Times*, 5 November 2006.

14 This section is based on Giustozzi (forthcoming) and on a personal communication with UN official, Kabul, March 2007.

15 Harm Ede Botje, 'We zitten darr goed', *Vrij Nederland*, 6 January 2007 courtesy of J. van den Zwan, Crisis States Research Centre, London).

16 Syed Mohsin Naqvi, 'Musharraf: Taliban gaining power', *CNN*, 20 July 2006; Zeeshan Haider, 'Unity, not games on Taliban, Pakistan urges Kabul', *Reuters*, 7 November 2006; Ahmed Rashid, 'Musharraf: stop aiding the Taliban', *Daily Telegraph*, 6 October 2006; 'President Musharaff's visit to Washington', *www.onlinenews.com.pk*, 27 September 2006; Ahmed Rashid, 'Accept defeat by Taliban, Pakistan tells NATO', *Daily Telegraph*, 30 November 2006; Ahmed Rashid, 'NATO commanders demand Pakistan close Taliban sanctuary', *Eurasia Insight*, 6 October 2006; Kristin Roberts, 'Gates seeks Pakistani help for NATO offensive', *Reuters*, 12 February 2007; Declan Walsh, 'Rice puts Musharraf under pressure to rein in Taliban militants', *Guardian*, 19 February 2007.

17 Syed Saleem Shahzad, 'Now Pakistan rounds on the Taliban', *Asia Times Online*, 2 September 2004; Ron Synovitz, 'Afghanistan: Pakistan hails capture of Taliban spokesman as breakthrough', *RFE/RL*, 5 October 2005; Declan Walsh and Bagarzai Saidan, 'Across the border from Britain's troops, Taliban rises again'; 'Pakistan arrests 140 Afghans', *RFE/RL Newsline*, 19 July 2006; 'Afghanistan frees 104 "Talibans" captured by Pakistan', *DPA*, 22 September 2006; 'Pakistan hands over Taliban suspects to Afghanistan', *Reuters*, 24 November 2006; 'Pakistan police arrest dozens of Taliban suspects', *Reuters*, 21 November 2006; 'Pakistan says arrests 500 Taliban this year', *Reuters*, 14 December 2006; Azhar Masood, '400 Taleban suspects held in Balochistan', *Arab News*, 19 January 2007; 'Bush to Musharraf: deal or no deal? White House pressures Pakistani leader to do more on terror', *CBS News*, 26 February 2007; personal communication with UN official,

March 2007.

18 Syed Saleem Shahzad, 'Afghanistan strikes back at Pakistan', *Asia Times Online*, 9 November 2006; 'Afghans among seven held over Quetta bomb blast', *AFP*, 22 December 2006.

19 See Coll (2004).

20 Cordesman (2007); Paul Watson, 'On the trail of the Taliban's support', *Los Angeles Times*, 24 December 2006, who claims to have seen DIA documents according to which ISI operatives were gathering information about US activities in Afghanistan. According to NATO sources, Pakistani volunteers captured in Afghanistan have provided plenty of details on the ISI structure of support for the Taliban (Ahmed Rashid, 'Musharraf: stop aiding the Taliban'); Schiewek (2006), p. 158.

21 Seth Jones, quoted in Declan Walsh, 'As Taliban insurgency gains strength and sophistication, suspicion falls on Pakistan', *Guardian*, 13 November 2006.

22 'Afghan situation a US policy failure, experts tell senators', *Daily Times*, 15 December 2006; David Montero, 'Attacks heat up Afghan-Pakistani border', *Christian Science Monitor*, 12 January 2007; personal communication with Pakistani journalist, Kabul, October 2006; personal communication with Afghan travellers to Quetta, Kabul, May 2006; Laura King, 'Pakistani city serves as a refuge for the Taliban', *Los Angeles Times*, 21 December 2006; Farhan Bokhari, 'Is Quetta Taliban's nerve centre?', *Gulf News Online*, 19 October 2003; Declan Walsh and Bagarzai Saidan, 'Across the border from Britain's troops, Taliban rises again'; Graeme Smith, 'Taliban plot new offensive against NATO', *Globe and Mail*, 18 January 2007; Paul Watson, 'On the trail of the Taliban's support'; David S. Cloud, 'U.S. says attacks are surging in Afghanistan', *New York Times*, 16 January 2007; David Rohde, 'G.I.s in Afghanistan on hunt, but now for hearts and minds', *New York Times*, 30 March 2004; 'Musharraf admits border problems', *BBC News*, 2 February 2007; 'Afghan border: Pakistan's struggle with the Taliban', *CBC News*, 5 December 2006 <http://www.cbc.ca/news/viewpoint/vp_edwards/20061205.html>; Syed Saleem Shahzad, 'Interview: Hamid Gul', *Asia Times Online*, 13 November 2001; Syed Saleem Shahzad, 'Taliban's trail leads to Pakistan', *Asia Times Online*, 13 December 2001; Syed Saleem Shahzad, 'Afghanistan's highway to hell', *Asia Times Online*, 25 January 2007; on the significance of the adoption of more traditional guerrilla tactics see also Jason Burke, 'Taliban plan to fight through winter to throttle Kabul', *Observer*, 29 October 2006; 'No indications Iran supplying weapons to Taliban', *Daily Times*, 12 February 2007.

23 Rubin (2007); Sayed Yaqub Ibrahimi, 'Taliban find unexpected arms source', *Afghan Recovery Report*, no. 206 (12 March 2006); 'Afghan officers arrested for smuggling weapons to Taliban', *Xinhua*, 21 September 2006; Guy Dinmore and Rachel Morarjee, 'To a second front? How Afghanistan could again be engulfed by civil war', *Financial Times*, 22 November 2006; Graeme Smith, 'The Taliban: knowing the enemy', *Globe and Mail*, 27

November 2006; Hamid Mir, 'The Taliban's new face'; 'Weapon smugglers should be arrested', *Hewaad*, 25 December 2006; Zulfiqar Ali, 'Kalashnikov prices shoot up', *Dawn*, 10 February 2007; Fisnik Abrashi, 'Gov't flounders in north Afghanistan', *Associated Press*, 27 February 2007; Senlis Council (2007), p. 32.

24 For a short review of Pakistani influence in Helmand, see Senlis Council (2006d), pp. 7 and 18; Françoise Chipaux, 'Les talibans font régner leur loi dans les provinces pachtounes du Sud', *Le Monde*, 7 October 2004.

25 Elizabeth Rubin, 'In the land of the Taliban'; Syed Saleem Shahzad, 'Pakistan reaches into Afghanistan', *Asia Times Online*, 3 October 2006; Ahmed Rashid, 'Accept defeat by Taliban, Pakistan tells NATO'; report on President Musharaff's visit to Washington, *www.onlinenews.com.pk*, 27 September 2006.

26 David Rohde, 'Iran is seeking more influence in Afghanistan', *New York Times*, 27 December 2006; Tahir (2007); 'Afghan rejects Iran's call to oust occupiers', *AFP*, 27 November 2006; Paul Watson, 'On the trail of the Taliban's support'; Connell and Nader (2006); Pamela Constable, 'Iran said to assist forces opposing Kabul government', *Washington Post*, 24 January 2002; 'Kanadahar official accuses Iran of arming commanders in Afghanistan', *AFP*, 21 January 2002; 'Iran seeking to draw western Afghanistan into its sphere of influence', *Associated Press*, 14 February 2006; Artie McConnell, 'Iranian conservatives seek to influence developments in Afghanistan; *Eurasia Insight*, 14 February 2002; Julian Borger, 'Surprising partners among Tehran's layer of alliances', *Guardian*, 10 February 2007; Graeme Smith, 'Tensions mount over Tehran's Afghan ambitions', *Globe and Mail*, 13 February 2007; Michael R. Gordon, 'U.S. says Iranian arms seized in Afghanistan', *New York Times*, 18 April 2007.

2
HOW AND WHY THE TALIBAN RECRUITED

2.1 HOW STRONG ARE THE TALIBAN?

Even sources like the US Armed Forces, NATO and the UN implicitly recognise a marked increase in the fighting force of the Taliban between 2002 and 2006. This is evident when estimates of the strength of the Taliban are compared year-on-year (see Table 1). In this author's opinion though, NATO and US sources tend to release very conservative estimates, often at odds with their own combat casualties assessments. These estimates are likely to reflect the number of insurgents active at any given time, rather than the total number of individuals who joined the insurgency. For analytical purposes an attempt has been made here to break down their estimates into core and local fighters. Note that 'local' does not refer just to the fact that such fighters were recruited locally, but to the predominance of local interests in their motivations (see 2.2 *Early recruitment*); a substantial number of 'hard-core' fighters were also recruited in the villages. Total figures tend to fluctuate a lot because of the seasonal mobilisation of part-time fighters, varying rates of movement across the border and other factors. Estimates of the number of 'hard-core' fighters recruited in the madaras of Pakistan show a greater degree of consistency. In 2004 US estimates were of some 1,000 'hard-core' insurgents inside Afghanistan, a figure which grew to 2–3,000 by 2004 and to 3–4,000 by 2006. UN sources put the estimate for local fighters in the south alone in 2006 at about 6,000. The hard-core combatants recruited away from the villages were doing two- to three-month shifts inside Afghanistan and passing the remaining time resting in Pakistan, spending between a fifth and half of their time at the battlefront, depending on many factors including their agreements with individual commanders. Local recruits would presumably spend most or all the time inside Afghanistan, but would not always be active militarily if the focus of operations was away from their home area. Although these local recruits were not always at the battlefront, they were easier to mobilise than those based in Pakistan. On this basis, the total number of combatants in the ranks of the Taliban and their allies must have reached around 17,000 men by 2006, with 6–10,000 active at any given time. Some Afghan sources were putting the figure as high as 40,000, but this seems to be out of line even with the Taliban's own claims. Of course, these numbers were supplemented by international volunteers and Pakistani Taliban. The numbers of the former appear to have fluctuated between less than a thousand and two thousand, apparently first declining until at least 2004 and then recovering in 2006 and possibly as early as 2005. The pool from which the latter were recruited appears to have numbered in the tens of thousands from 2004, when the conflict in Waziristan started. The importance of the Pakistani Taliban was highlighted when in late 2006 a major upsurge in cross-border attacks took place, following peace deals between militants and Pakistani authorities in Waziristan. According to US intelligence sources, cross-border attacks in Khost and Paktika rose from forty in the two months preceding the agreement to 140 in the two months following it. Pakistani volunteers had, however, been playing an important role in the conflict since at least 2005. A cluster of twenty-five villages in Pakistani Pashtunistan reportedly lost over 100 young men to the jihad in Afghanistan up to the beginning of 2007, while sources from the ranks of the Pakistani Taliban indicated that 175 militants from South Waziristan alone lost their lives fighting in Afghanistan just in 2005–6. During just the first two months of 2007 the bodies of forty-five militants were repatriated to Pakistan. Since an estimated two-thirds of the Waziristan militants are reportedly based in North Waziristan and militants are also based elsewhere in Pakistan, the number of Pakistani martyrs in the new Afghan jihad must be running into several hundreds or more than 20 per cent of total insurgent losses.[1]

Initially foreign volunteers represented a significant share of the ranks of the insurgents. As the ranks of the Taliban expanded, the incidence of the foreign volunteer component lost importance, even if some of them seem to have continued to play advisory roles, accompanying Taliban commanders. When Taliban and foreign insurgents operated together, the commanders were always Afghans, at least according to the Taliban. From the beginning the foreign volunteers were mostly active in the south-east (Khost, Paktika) and in the east (Kunar, Nuristan). At the beginning of 2004, for example, the volunteers still constituted a third of the Taliban's strength in Paktika.[2]

	2002	2003	2004	2005	2006
Estimates by international sources					
Core (active)		1,000		2,000–3,000	3,000–4,000
Non-core				3,000–4,000	4,000–7,000
Estimates by author					
Core	3,000	4,000	4,500	5,500	7,000
core (active)	*500–1,500*	*800–2,000*	*1,200–2,500*	*2,000–3,000*	*3,000–4,000*
core madrasa-recruited	*3,000*	*3,700*	*3,700*	*4,400*	*5,500*
core village-recruited	*0*	*300*	*800*	*1,100*	*1,500*
Non-core village-recruited	1,000	3,000	5,000	7,000	10,000
average active (core + non-core)	*500–2,000*	*1,500–4,000*	*3,000–5,500*	*5,000–7,000*	*6,000–10,000*
Total	4,000	7,000	9,500	12,500	17,000
Foreign volunteers	1,500	1,000	700	1,200	2,000
Pakistani Taliban				40,000	40,000

Table 1. Estimates of the strength of the Taliban.

Sources: press reports, NATO sources, ISAF sources, US military sources, UN sources.

To estimate even roughly what degree of support the Taliban might have at the national level is extremely difficult. To this purpose a few opinion polls were carried out in 2005–6, but using polls to assess the political views of the population in a conflict zone is a quite controversial approach. It is unlikely that villagers in the war zone, aware of the possible fate of supporters of the Taliban, when approached by unknown pollsters would give honest answers to questions such as 'do you support the government?'. It is worth noting that most pollsters declared their inability to carry out polls in some provinces, usually including at least Zabul and Uruzgan, the two main strongholds of the Taliban at the time. When the sample of polled individuals was made available, it seemed very strongly biased towards individuals with at least some education, more likely to be opposed to the Taliban than the rest of the population. In the BBC/ABC poll of October 2006 53 per cent of the sampled interviewees had received at least some education and 59 per cent were literate, a much higher percentage than that usually estimated for the population as a whole (28 per cent). Only 27 per cent of the interviewees with a job were farmers or farm labourers and 7 per cent were unemployed, whereas government figures place unemployment at 33 per cent of the workforce and people employed in the agricultural sector at 56 per cent. Five per cent were police and soldiers (0.6 per cent of the workforce in reality), who would certainly be expected to express support for the government. Fourteen per cent were managers and executives, another category unlikely to sympathise with the Taliban and obviously greatly over-represented. In the World Opinion poll of January 2006 only 36.8 per cent of the sample was Pashtun, as opposed to the obviously overrepresented Tajiks (38.8 per cent), who were much less likely to sympathise with the Taliban; 50 per cent of the sample were literate (as opposed to 28 per cent in the population). Four of thirty-four provinces were not covered, but the poll did not specify which ones.[3]

Still, on the basis of polls like this, NATO sources claimed in 2006 that just 10 per cent of the population in the south supported the insurgents, whereas 20 per cent supported the government and the rest were sitting on the fence. However, local authorities and journalists travelling to the provinces affected by the insurgency had very different views about popular support for the Taliban. In the case of Uruzgan, Dutch sources were estimating that the Taliban controlled

80 per cent of the province, while the Australians claimed that no more than 40 per cent was under the control of government/foreign forces. The former governor of that province, Jan Mohammed, stated that the Taliban could count on the support of the population. The situation was similar in Helmand and Zabul at least (see 2.6 *Recruiting local communities*), and a British official admitted to a Pakistani journalist that the majority of the population in the south-west supported the Taliban.[4]

Clearly, while there is no question that although the insurgency initially had a small constituency, the Taliban successfully expanded their recruitment base from 2003 onwards. Numbers, of course, do not tell the whole story. To understand the expansion of the ranks of the insurgency, we have to examine in detail how the recruitment base widened between 2002 and 2006.

2.2 EARLY RECRUITMENT

The first reports of the Taliban's attempt to create in an organised way a rear support area in the NWFP and in Baluchistan surfaced in December 2001. As early as March 2002 a leader of the Taliban, Mullah Obaidullah Akhund, was reported to have issued a call to arms, while other middle rank leaders were already trying to use nationalist feelings in order to mobilise support against the 'occupiers'. Other sources within the Movement give a somewhat different, although not necessarily inconsistent, account of the start of the insurgency. According to these sources, sometime in the first half of 2002 Mullah Omar would have contacted his old commanders and asked them to carry out a census of their rank-and-file, finding out who was still alive. He then proceeded to launch a recruitment drive among madrasa students in Baluchistan and in Karachi, despatching Mullah Dadullah and Mawlawi Sadiq Hameed to find fresh flesh for the battlefield. A third prominent Talib commander, Hafiz Majeed, was allegedly sent into Afghanistan to seek support among tribal leaders and elders. Whatever the exact timing of the call to arms, a small army of recruiters was soon systematically visiting refugee camps (particularly Girdijangle in the Chagai Hills), madaras, mosques, social gatherings of various types and Pakistani Pashtun villages throughout the region of Quetta, signing up volunteers. Training camps, mostly mobile ones, were then set up around Quetta to train small groups of insurgents. A separate recruitment effort was likely underway in the NWFP. Nonetheless, the appeal was initially not very successful. It appears that relatively few of the 'old Taliban' rushed to join the new jihad. A group of twenty-two fighters interviewed by a journalist in Ghazni at the end of the summer of 2005 included just two veterans of the pre-2002 period, although by the time of the interview some of the 'old Taliban' might also have died in the fighting. In remote areas inside Afghanistan some groups of stray Taliban reactivated themselves towards the end of 2002 or early 2003 (see 4.2 *Rooting out government presence*), but that was about it. As a result, the age of the fighters mostly ranged between twenty to twenty-five years, with commanders being somewhat older at thirty to forty. Only among the top leaders were the 'old Taliban' present in strength, in fact accounting for all of the ten to twelve members of the Leadership Council (see 2.5 *Taliban, tribes and elders* and 3.3 *Command structure*). However, even those 'old Taliban' who did not directly join the insurgency at the beginning might have done so later or in any case contributed to spread pro-Taliban feelings among the population. In Uruzgan in the late summer of 2002, for example, many Taliban were uneasily waiting for further developments in their villages, sometimes continuing to claim their allegiance to the Movement, other times trying to recycle themselves as pro-government and even pro-American. Similarly, the presence of many inactive Taliban was reported in Farah province. In the end, the attitude of the authorities and the changing circumstances of Afghanistan would prove decisive in orienting the decisions of the 'old Taliban'.[5]

Throughout 2002–6 Pakistani madaras continued to provide an inexhaustible flow of new recruits as many Afghan families continued to send their children to study there. The absence of prestigious madaras in Afghan territory and the financially advantageous conditions offered by some Pakistani madaras convinced Afghan families to send their children across the border. However, from 2003 onwards recruitment started following other paths too. An obvious one in the Afghan context was kinship ties, which became a privileged channel of recruitment. It appears, however, that the biggest numbers came through the support of the clergy and through enlisting community support in specific areas (see 2.6 *Recruiting local communities*).[6]

What are the underlying factors of the Taliban's appeal among the Pashtun tribal youth? The interpretation of Imran Gul, programme director of the Sustainable Participation Development Program, an NGO based in Banu, just outside North Waziristan, applies to the NWFP, but appears to have some validity for Afghanistan as well. Gul believes that the tribal system is in crisis and that it can no longer provide 'peace, income, a sense of purpose, a social network' to the local youth, who then turn to radical movements (collectively known as the Pakistani Taliban) as the only outlet where they can express their frustration and earn the prestige once offered by the tribal system. Officials working in the region support this view, claiming that the youth 'oppose the current tribal system because they know that this is not … harnessing their potential'. Military incursions in the tribal areas further undermined the influence of the elders in the NWFP and might have had the same result in Afghanistan. A Pakistani official from South Waziristan expressed similar opinions: 'Military actions and policy have contributed to the anarchical situation that pro-Taliban militants are more than happy to fill. Their demonstrated ability to restore order, prosecute criminals and dispense speedy justice was welcomed by many civilians fed up with violence and insecurity.' The conclusion of an ICG analyst is that 'fear of the militants, combined with resentment against a corrupt administration and draconian laws, has contributed to local acquiescence of Taliban-style governance.' The sidelining of the Waziri tribal elders and the emergence of the clergy in a prominent political role resulted for the first time in the recruitment of members of rival tribes under a common banner for long-term political action. It should be added that the success of the local Taliban was favoured by the implicit complicity of the Pakistani administration of the NWFP, which only allowed pro-Taliban and Islamist political groups to operate in the area, preventing secular groups from competing with them.[7] In Afghanistan the legitimacy of tribal and village elders was weakened by the war and by the emergence of armed strongmen who often tried to replace the elders, without entirely succeeding.[8] Moreover, the youth who grew up in the Pakistani refugee camps were much less likely to be respectful of the tribal elders. Anecdotal evidence suggests that the disruption caused by Afghan militias, police and foreign troops contributed to further weaken tribal and local elders. At the same time the difficulty of the tribal system (where it still existed) or of the rural economy to cope with war, post-war, large scale migration and resettlement, together with the uncertainty about the medium- and long-term future, led many families to seek a diversification of their sources of revenue and influence. Hence an increase in the number of children sent to the Pakistani religious madaras to become mullahs or to the cities to seek employment, both cases contributing to further weaken the influence of the elders over the youth. These alienated youths provided fertile recruitment ground for the Taliban.[9]

2.3 HARD-CORE, MERCENARIES AND OTHERS

Allegations that the Taliban were fielding a largely 'mercenary' force abounded in the press and in the statements of both the Afghan government and the foreign contingents. Reports and estimates suggested that most Taliban guerrillas were little short of mercenaries earning between US$100 and US$350 per month, depending on the region. That would be at least on a par with soldiers of the ANA and possibly as much as three times their income. The Taliban, by contrast, presented their payments as an indemnity for the families of the combatants, who would otherwise be deprived of their source of income. Indeed, the idea that the Taliban are mostly a mercenary force is at odds with strong evidence showing the commitment of Taliban fighters and their readiness to fight to the last man, as well

The first two categories can be said to be part of the 'hard-core' Taliban, while the remaining two are both 'non-core' in character (see 2.1 *How strong are the Taliban?*). The exact mix of the various types of insurgents varied greatly from province to province. For example, in areas far from the border, the percentage of madrasa-recruited fighters coming from Pakistan was unsurprisingly lower. Dutch sources estimated that in 2006 only 2 per cent of Taliban fighters in Uruzgan were not originally from that province. The rest of the 300–500 hard-core insurgents estimated to be there (20 per cent of the total) must therefore have been composed of hard-core Taliban recruited in the villages. Similarly in Helmand the total for the hard-core component was estimated at 20 per cent or 250–350 men. In Zabul a source put the hard-core component at 10 per cent, although this appears an underestimate. On average, by 2006 village jihadists might have accounted for perhaps 15–25 per cent of the active fighting strength of the Taliban at any given time, with madrasa recruits accounting for around 25 per cent, local allies for 40–50 per cent and mercenaries for another 10–15 per cent.[14]

2.4 THE ROLE OF THE CLERGY

The clergy as such was not one of the constitutive components of the insurgency in its early days. Most of the leaders of the Movement of the Taliban were indeed mullahs, but there is little evidence that initially a significant number of members of the clergy openly supported the rebels inside Afghanistan. However, the situation changed rather rapidly in many parts of the country, not least because of obvious ideological contiguities between the Taliban and the more conservative components of the Afghan clergy.[15] The Taliban regime had relied on them to control the country and gather information from the villages.[16] There were some sectors of the clergy, such as Sufi Tariqas, which were either politically indifferent or even pro-government and resented the prevarication of the new generation of Deobandi-influenced young mullahs. However, by the early twenty-first century Deobandism influenced probably the majority of the

Afghan clergy, particularly in the areas bordering Pakistan, as most mullahs had been trained in Pakistani madaras aligned with this fundamentalist-leaning school. The old Sufis were in decline. This can be seen as the culmination of a process of politicisation of the Afghan Ulema, which started in the nineteenth century and played to the advantage of the Movement of the Taliban, providing it with a natural constituency within Afghanistan. Whenever surveys of the opinions of the clergy were attempted, they found that regardless of their attitude towards the insurgency, they were hostile to the presence of foreign troops and unfriendly towards the government.[17]

The importance of clerical networks goes beyond the encouragement that they might have given to potential village recruits of the Taliban. In rural Afghanistan, due to the fragmentation of the population in multiple and often rival local communities, the clergy is often the only supra-communitarian network, particularly in remote rural areas. Its role in promoting collective action beyond the community level is therefore crucial.[18] Even the pre-1980s 'fragmented networks' had played an important role in the mobilisation of the jihad movement of the 1978–92 period, bypassing the segmentarity of local communities and allowing it to organise at least alliances at the sub-provincial level. By the 1990s these local networks were showing the tendency to coalesce into wider ones.[19] This was probably a result of the shift which occurred during the 1980s. Madrasa education declined in Afghanistan, where most students would have attended local schools, and moved to Pakistan, where students from different regions would meet and be socialised in each single madrasa.[20] Moreover, many young Afghans growing up in Pakistan were socialised in a non-tribal and more religious environment. It is also likely that the shared Deobandi background played an important role in increasing the homogeneity of the clergy, making political communication and alliances easier.

The first clerical networks to start supporting the Taliban appeared to have been those located in Zabul, where they started supporting the insurgency as early as 2003. At that time the district governor of Shah Joy, one of the districts where government presence was stronger due to the fact that it is crossed by the main highway, estimated that the clergy of 25 mosques and madaras were supporting the Taliban within his area of responsibility. By the admission of the provincial governor, by 2006 'Zabul's religious leaders all supported the Taliban. In northern Helmand the first signs that part of the clergy was preaching jihad against the government and Americans emerged in the summer of 2004. A similar pattern was reported at least for Ghazni and Paktika, although the dating is uncertain. In other parts of southern Afghanistan, such as Kandahar province, the mullahs started openly supporting the Taliban later, but by 2006 such support was widespread in the rural districts. Only within Kandahar city did most mullahs remain pro-government. The Afghan security forces were well aware of this and in July 2006 carried out raids in mosques and madaras in several districts, arresting some 150 people, of which twenty-five were then detained. [21]

There were important pockets of resistance to the trend. In Paktia (Paktya) and Khost, the clergy remained hostile to the Taliban well into 2006, due to the strength of local Sufi networks. The conservative Tablighi networks do not appear to have supported the Taliban either. However, the shift of the clergy towards supporting the insurgency was not limited to the south and parts of the south-east. During 2006 reports emerged that the mullahs of Wardak were beginning to express support for the Taliban. Indeed by 2006 the presence of mullahs urging the believers to join the jihad against the government and the foreigners was reported even in Kabul's mosques. The mullahs who railed against the moral corruption dominating Kabul included some who had previously supported members of the government coalition. Mullahs preaching against the government and the foreigners were reported as far as Takhar and Badakhshan provinces in north-eastern Afghanistan. In Badakhshan, the Taliban seem to have approached mullahs from the southern districts of Jurm, Yamgan, Keran-e Munjan and Warduj and even to have invited them to Pakistan for discussions.[22]

The Taliban enhanced the role of their allies among the clergy by eliminating or intimidating into silence pro-government mullahs. In Kandahar the killings of mullahs started in the summer of 2003. Between June and July three were killed in the city. The campaign to assassinate pro-government religious figures continued unabated after 2003 and Kandahar remained very much the focus of the assassination campaign. Of twenty clerics assassinated between the summers of 2005 and 2006, twelve were from Kandahar. Another forty were wounded countrywide over the same period, and countless received threats. The focus on Kandahar is probably linked to the concentration in this city of pro-government mullahs, as well as to the fact that in rural areas few mullahs could afford to ignore the death threats. The survivors had three options. They could rely on the protection of armed guards, if they were influential enough to deserve government protection or could afford it. Alternatively, they could live in hiding, which suited the Taliban because it prevented them from preaching. Finally, they could flee to safer places. As a result, the residual influence of pro-government mullahs was almost obliterated in the areas affected by the insurgency.[23]

2.5 TALIBAN, TRIBES AND ELDERS

Some analysts as well as Afghan commentators have seen a tribal dimension in the insurgency, in particular identifying the Ghilzai tribes as the main source of support for the Neo-Taliban. This interpretation of the causes of the insurgency rests on the alleged near-domination of the leadership of the Taliban by Ghilzais, especially the Hotak tribe. This, however, is incorrect, at least as far as the Neo-Taliban movement of 2003–6 was concerned. As Table 2 shows, in 2003–4 the Rahbari Shura (Leadership Council), which includes the main political military leaders of the Neo-Taliban, was not dominated by Ghilzais. If anything, the Durrani tribes were better represented. The 'Ghilzai insurgency' interpretation seems to have been popular within the ranks of US armed forces in Afghanistan, who were reported by some of their NATO allies as seeing the

Rahbari Shura 2003	*Rahbari Shura 2004*	
Name	*Name*	*Tribal background*
Mullah Omar	Mullah Omar	Hotak (Ghilzai)
Mullah Obaidullah	Mullah Obaidullah	Alkozai (Durrani)
Saifullah Mansoor		Sahak tribe (Ghilzai)
Mullah Dadullah	Mullah Dadullah	Kakar (Ghurghusht)
Akthar Mohammad Osmani	Akthar Mohammad Osmani	Ishaqzai (Durrani)
Jalaluddin Haqqani	Jalaluddin Haqqani	Zadran (Karlanri)
Mullah Baradar	Mullah Baradar	Popolzai (Durrani)
Mullah Rasul		Noorzai(?) (Durrani)
Hafiz Abdul Majid	Hafiz Abdul Majid	Noorzai (Durrani)
Mullah Abdur Razzaq*	Mullah Abdur Razzaq	Achakzai (Durrani)
Akhtar Mohammad Mansoor		Ishaqzai (Durrani)
	Amir Khan Muttaqi	Suleimankhel (Ghilzai)
	Mullah Mohammed Hassan Rehmani	Achakzai (Durrani)
	Qudratullah Jamal	Andar (Ghilzai)
	Mullah Abdul Kabir	Zadran (Karlanri)

Table 2. Composition of the Rahbari Shura and tribal background of its members (all members were Pashtuns by ethnicity).

* It is not clear whether this was Abdur Razzaq Nafiz, who was later killed by the Americans, or Abdur Razzaq Akhundzada, who was member of the Shura in 2004.

Sources: G. Smith, 'The Taliban: Knowing the enemy', *Globe and Mail*, 27 November 2006; 'Taliban Announce Creation of Council to Help "Evict" Leadership in Afghanistan', *RFE/RL Newsline*, 25 June 2003; Tsentral'nyi Bank RF, 'Prilozhenie n. 2, K ukazanniyu operativnogo kharaktera ot 20 avgusta 2002 goda n. 116-T, Obnovlennye spiski lits, imeyushikh otnoshenie k Afganskomy dvizheniyu Taliban'; Sayyid Massoud, *Posht-e purdeh kasi hasht!*, Kabul: Ahmad Printing Press, 2003.

Ghilzai tribe as synonymous with the Taliban, without any attempt to differentiate.[24]

More important, the pattern according to which local communities divided up into pro-government and pro-Taliban did not follow a strict tribal logic. The Taliban were ready to accept anybody who shared their views and accepted their rules, regardless of ethnicity and tribe. Taliban teams were always mixing together individuals with different tribal backgrounds. Clearly, the Taliban did not want to present themselves as aligned with a particular tribe or community. This made it easier for them to move across tribal territories without antagonising the locals, but at the same time was also a way of advertising the Movement as above inter-community rivalry. All those who had supported the Taliban regime and had been marginalised afterwards were prime targets for recruitment, regardless of their tribal background. Even if an estimated 95 per cent of the members were Pashtuns, they did try to recruit members of other ethnic groups as well. In Kahmard district (Bamian) support for the Taliban was reported among a number of small and marginalised Tajik armed groups. In Ghazni by 2006 the Taliban were trying with some success to reactivate groups of Hazara supporters who had cooperated with their regime in 1998–2001. Similarly, the assassination of a German NGO worker in Sar-i Pul in March 2007 is likely to have been carried out by a small gang of former Taliban collaborationists in the north. The presence of pro-Taliban pockets was also reported from 2005–6 in the southern districts of Ghor, where the population is largely Tajik Aimaq. As far as Pashtun tribes are concerned, the 'winner takes all' approach adopted at the end of 2001 ended up creating fissures even within the Popolzais, Karzai's own tribe. In the Shah Wali Kwot district of Kandahar, former collaborators of the Taliban were completely marginalised socially and politically in 2001 and later joined the Taliban to fight. Even among the Achakzais a significant number of Taliban could be found, despite the traditional enmity of many Achakzai communities with the largely pro-Taliban Noorzais. It is true that the tribal distribution of pro-Taliban communities was very uneven. Many were found among the western Ghilzais, who also felt marginalised in terms of spoils distribution. Other southern tribes within which support for the Taliban was widespread included the Kakar and the Tarin, but also many communities belonging to the Durrani tribes were drawn towards the insurgency, first and foremost the Noorzais of Kandahar (see 2.6 *Recruiting local communities*). The uneven participation of the tribes in the insurgency was the result of the tribal politics of the government and local authorities, rather than a conscious targeting by the Taliban (see 2.6 *Recruiting local communities* and 1.2 *'Rebuilding' the Afghan state*). One good reason for this is that in southern Afghanistan, and much of the south-east too, tribal structures had long disintegrated and tribes had lost their cohesion, if they ever had any.[25]

Some US sources alleged that cooperation between the Taliban and the tribes occurred at the higher level, implying the involvement of tribal leaders. Whether this is correct or not, it cannot be construed to mean that the leaders of the Ghilzais or of any other tribe/confederation supported the Taliban, for the simple reason that such 'grand' tribal leaders do not exist. Outside some tribes of the south-east and east (in any case not the Ghilzais) tribal leadership occurs at the clan and sub-tribe level if at all. There is instead evidence that certainly in at least some areas of Afghanistan elders and secular notables welcomed the Taliban in order to gain support in local struggles against communities connected to the government and old-time rivals (see 2.6 *Recruiting local communities*). However, in general relations between elders and Neo-Taliban have not been good. Even in Mullah Omar's native village of Sangisar (Kandahar), the leaders resisted their activities in the area and tried to limit their presence as much as possible. There might be several reasons for this, including the fact that Taliban field commanders were young and elders might have resented their role (or *vice versa*). Moreover, many Taliban fighters and commanders were mullahs or trainee mullahs, a fact which is also unlikely to endear them to the elders, who could easily see them as rivals for influence. Deobandi mullahs and elders refer to alternative systems of legitimisation, one based on residual tribal traditions, control over wealth/land and community management skills, the other based on religion/'ideology' and skills in building bridges among local communities. Indeed, where elders remained strong and in control, they usually actively worked to prevent the infiltration of the Taliban. This is typically the case of the south-eastern provinces of Paktia and Khost, where with a few exceptions as of October 2006 the insurgents were still unable to find hospitality in the villages. In this area the tribal leaders were still able to impose tribal decisions and punish transgressors, particularly among the Mangals (see 2.6 *Recruiting local communities*). A number of anecdotes suggest that often elders have been instrumental in mobilising local opposition to the Taliban. For example, in January 2006 a group of Achakzai villagers in Spin Boldak (Kandahar) forced a group of Taliban out of their village after a gun battle. In another example, the strongman Haji Lalai Mama of Loy Karez village in Kandahar province gathered together a village defence to keep the Taliban away. In Panjwai Haji Lalai tried to do the same by sponsoring an anti-Taliban movement, but was instead forced to flee by the insurgents and had to seek refuge in Kandahar city. Even in Musa Qala, where local authorities tried to portray the elders who signed a truce agreement with the British as indistinguishable from the Taliban, strong contrasts were reported between the latter and the elders once the truce collapsed. Occasionally government authorities seem to have realised the role of elders as potential allies. For example, in the autumn of 2003 the governor of Zabul, Hafizullah Hashem, created a commission to work with the elders of Dai Chopan, a Taliban stronghold. The offer was to trade off government support (provision of services etc.) with allegiance to the Taliban. In order for the tribal elders to play a significant political role, they had to be either incorporated in state-sponsored structures, such as the Peace Strengthening Commission, or mobilised from above to participate in tribal assemblies. However, the inability to provide security at the local level and the general weakness of the subnational administration prevented the government from successfully mobilising potential support among the elders.[26]

Despite the fact that the elders in general showed little enthusiasm for supporting the insurgents, the Taliban would first of all approach the elders in order to be granted the right to enter tribal territory and the villages. If successful, they would establish themselves in the territory and then either work with the elders or gradually marginalise them. In certain areas and on certain issues, such as the opposition to foreign presence or to the eradication of the poppies, the elders were aligned with the Taliban. In areas like these, the Taliban were ready to allow them a say. This seems to have been common in northern Helmand. For example, the elders of Musa Qala were able to negotiate a truce between the British and the Taliban in October 2006. Friction occurred at times between Taliban and elders, but the local commanders of the Taliban most of the time managed to contain it. There and at least in Zabul too, but probably in Uruzgan and parts of Kandahar as well, elders found that the Taliban were the only force which could help express their grudges against the government. Some reports suggested that the widespread use of air power and its side effects contributed to push many elders to side with the insurgents.[27]

If unsuccessful in being allowed into a village's territory or when facing resistance from a section of the elders, the insurgents would start targeting elders in a campaign of intimidation and murder, usually accusing the victims of being US spies. The most famous example of a notable opposing the Taliban and paying the price for it is that of Qari Baba, former governor of Ghazni under Rabbani, who was assassinated in March 2006 after announcing that he was taking over the security of Andar district in order to defeat the insurgency. The elders often found it difficult to oppose the Taliban's onslaught, once the latter became able to concentrate large numbers of their men in a small area. On the whole, it would seem that the Taliban's carrot-and-stick tactics to bring the elders in line were quite successful. During the Presidential elections of 2004, none of the village and tribal elders of the districts of Atghar, Shamulzay, Shinkay, Suri and Nawbahar (Zabul) accepted to take part in the organisation of the electoral process. Three elders from Arghandab district, who agreed to do so, were later executed by the Taliban. Even in Panjwai under the occupation of Canadian and government troops (November 2006), when a delegation including the Minister of Rural Development and the Deputy of the UN Special Representative travelled to Kandahar to meet the elders, several of them refused to attend the meeting. After Operation Baaz Tsuka in December 2006, despite occupying the ground militarily the Canadians could not identify the local elders in order to arrange with them the distribution of aid. In general, the majority of elders appear to have been sensitive to the local balance of force and supported the Taliban whenever the authorities seemed to be unable to control territory. In response to this problem, NATO forces planned the deployment of police forces in the newly freed villages, strengthened by ANA strongholds, to work together as an early warning system against attempts to infiltrate Kandahar.[28]

2.6 RECRUITING LOCAL COMMUNITIES

NATO sources acknowledged a dramatic increase in the number of locally recruited fighters during 2006, even if in September 2006 NATO sources estimated that still 40 per cent of insurgents were coming straight from Pakistan. This was the result of a trend which had started much earlier, during 2003–4 when the Taliban were infiltrating into Afghan territory. Despite having been a mainly southern-based movement since its inception, after 2001 the Taliban did not particularly focus their efforts to infiltrate Afghanistan on any particular region. They started at about the same time all along the Pakistan border, with the south lagging slightly behind the south-east and the east. They met, however, with different degrees of success.[29]

a) *The south-east*

The military effort was initially strongest in the south-east, probably due to the local leadership and charisma of expert guerrilla leaders like Jalaluddin Haqqani, who had played an important role in the jihad of the 1980s. However, much of the south-east turned out to be a not so welcoming place for the insurgents. By 2006 they had only been able to find sufficient sympathy to establish a support infrastructure in Ghazni province, the south-eastern districts of Paktika, like Barmal and Terwah (Gomal), and the Zurmat district of Paktia. Paktia and Khost remained largely hostile to the rebels, mainly due to the strong opposition of the tribal leaders (see 2.5 *Taliban, tribes and elders*), even if by then there were signs that the support of the tribal leadership for Karzai and the government was waning because of its inability to provide security. The fact that no particular tribe or individual dominated the local authorities suggested the emergence of disgruntled or alienated communities (see 4.6 *Exploiting divisions among communities*). The majority of the few local insurgents seemed to have a Hizb-i Islami background more than a Taliban one. Using his own personal influence among the Zadran tribe and the madrasa network he built in the 1980s, Haqqani was able to maintain a relatively high degree of violence in the districts populated by this tribe. By the end of the summer of 2006 his men were beginning to threaten the road connecting Gardez to Khost, and crossing the mountainous Zadran territory started becoming dangerous. Still, he had not been able to establish real strongholds there. The fact that that road, which had been nearly impassable to Soviet and government troops in the 1980s, was regularly open until at least 2005 and still not closed although somewhat dangerous in 2006 is a clear sign of the weak penetration of the insurgency until then. However, the relentless attacks across the border with Pakistan were by early 2007 beginning to dent local opposition to the Taliban in some districts of Khost province.[30]

By contrast, the areas of the south-east where the influence of the tribal leaderships was weaker and that of the clergy stronger, such as southern Ghazni, much of Paktika and Zurmat of Paktia, saw a much more rapid expansion of Taliban influence. Here the mainstay of Taliban recruitment was the local conservative religious networks, which openly supported the insurgents, but there is evidence that support for the Taliban spread well beyond the clerics and their immediate followers. Unsurprisingly, the Taliban established their influence first where the government was weaker. Central-eastern Paktika, which is also on the border with Pakistan, was one of the first areas to fall under them. Although Paktika was heavily infiltrated by non-Afghan volunteers, according to US officers 'everybody' was fighting against their troops. One explanation might be

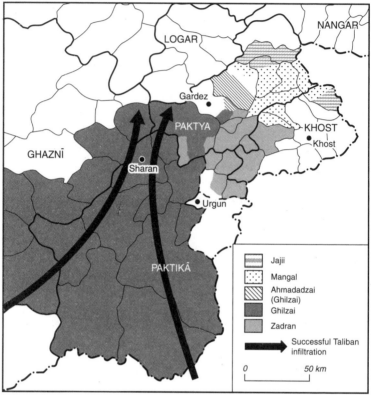

Map 3. Main tribes of south-eastern Afghanistan.
Source: Tribal Liaison Office, Kabul.

that the local population had been turned against the government by the mistreatment inflicted by the local authorities. Southern Ghazni, slightly more remote from the border, followed in 2004. By 2005–6 even eastern Ghazni was falling under the influence of the Taliban. During the summer of 2006 locals were reporting that the population was increasingly sympathising with the Taliban, even if in most cases they did not dare to openly side with them. At about the same time recruitment of locals started. Local support was acquired by such actions as eliminating a notorious local bandit, Bismillah Khan, who had been active on the main highway. In 2006 the government presence had been sufficiently weakened in northern Paktika too (Jajii) and, had it not been for the significant US military presence there, the region appeared well on its way to falling to the insurgents.[31]

b) *The south*

It was, however, in the south, despite the initial military weakness and inexperience of the insurgents, that the Neo-Taliban were most successful. In Kandahar and parts of Helmand and Uruzgan, Karzai's associates and allies with their militias had acted as a bulwark against the penetration of the Taliban (see 1.2 *'Rebuilding' the Afghan state*). However, the same men and their militias drove their local rivals over to the opposition by systematically marginalising them from all positions of power and then harassing them. Communities and individuals who had supported the Taliban, but even some that had not, feared that their tribal enemies might turn the government and the foreign contingents against them. 'Bad tips' by local informers, who were trying to cast their local rivals as Taliban and direct the security agencies or the foreign troops against them, appear to have been given quite frequently. The Taliban then appeared as the only protection available.[32]

This, for example, was the case of many among the Noorzais of Kandahar, who during the Taliban regime had been able to wrest control of the key border post of Spin Boldak from the rival Achakzais. With the fall of the Taliban, rival tribal militias from the two tribes confronted each other in Spin Boldak for some time. By the end of 2001, however, the Achakzais had gained decisive supremacy through their coalition with Gul Agha Shirzai, an ally of President Karzai and key power-broker in Kandahar (see 1.2 *'Rebuilding' the Afghan state*). Control of Spin Boldak was handed over to Achakzai militia leaders.[33] Now in control of the border police and extracting illegal taxes from travellers, they would also use their newly-found power to harass their old rivals and to brand them as Taliban, effectively pushing them over to the opposition. Having started in

Spin Boldak, the conflict spread to Panjwai district in 2006, where much of the population also belongs to the two tribes. The vehicle of the 'contagion' was the Achakzai-controlled border police, which was dispatched from Spin Boldak to contain Taliban infiltration in Panjwai, arousing the hostility of local Noorzais who were aware of its leader Abdul Razik's record in fighting other Noorzais in Spin Boldak. After Razik's border militia was defeated, police and ANA were called in to fight the 'insurgents', pushing Panjwai's Noorzais further into the arms of the Taliban. The Taliban took care to appoint a Noorzai as their field commander in Panjwai, facilitating the incorporation of the disgruntled villagers.[34]

In Zabul the recruitment of locals started no later than 2003. The recruits were Hotak and Tokhi Ghilzais (the two largest local tribes), opposed to the Kabul-sponsored Durrani by a long-running feud. In 2002 President Karzai had dispatched his nephew (a Durrani) to Zabul as chief of police, antagonising the locals. As the situation in Zabul started deteriorating, due to the infiltration of the Taliban and to inter-tribal feuding, Karzai, towards the end of 2003, replaced governor Hamidullah Tokhi, a former local commander and a Ghilzai, with one of his Durrani protégés from Kandahar, Hafizullah Hashem. As a result, Tokhi's men stopped fighting for the government, while Hashem could only bring a limited number of his own men from Kandahar, whose presence moreover was seen by the locals as further antagonism. By the end of 2003 five of Zabul's seven districts were under the control of the Taliban, leaving only the areas around the main highway under the influence of the government.[35]

In Uruzgan, the conflict initially opposed mainly Ghilzai and Noorzai to Popolzais, Barakzais and some Achakzai communities. However, several Achakzai communities in Gezab and in the northern part of Khas Uruzgan also joined the opposition to the Popolzai provincial rulers, who could count on Karzai's support. Some Moghol communities between Khas Uruzgan and Chora, who call themselves Barakzais, were also controlled by the insurgents. Jan Mohammed had a reputation of being an ineffective administra-

mobilised tribesmen from Gezab against him. Qudus Khan was killed in the fighting.[37]

Similar conflicts also developed in neighbouring districts, such as Kijran (later to become part of Daikundi province), where in 2003 district governor Abdur Rahman Khan was reportedly harassing local communities with his arbitrary behaviour and tax collection. In Char Chena it was the governor Toren Amanullah who collected taxes and had prisoners complained of ill-treatment. Later the two fought over the control of Kijran. The employment of tribally based militias to fight the Taliban compounded the problem. The Barakzai militia of Nisar Ahmad, for example, had occupied Tarin Kwot at the end of 2001 as the Taliban were fleeing. They proved very useful to Jan Mohammed in securing the surroundings of the provincial capital, but at the price of alienating the population of such places as Balochi Valley, north of Tarin Kwot, which became Taliban strongholds. The farther from Tarin Kwot, the more difficult it proved for Jan Mohammed to control the conflict he himself had started. Some of these districts, like Shahid-i Hassas and Gezab, fell completely into the hands of the Taliban. The power bloc created by Jan Mohammed survived his departure, not least because of the support of US Special Forces and of President Karzai himself. In early 2007 the militiamen of the district governor of Dihrawud clashed with the special reserve police force, losing two men. In revenge the district officials reportedly ordered the killing of the head of the special reserve and one of his men. Special Forces allegedly prevented him from being tried as he was one of their allies. In Tarin Kwot Jan Mohammed's nephew and chief of police, Matiullah, maintained a powerful and well-funded 1,000-strong militia even after his sacking. Within the administration of Tarin Kwot and among US Special Forces Matiullah maintained strong support as the most committed enemy of the Taliban and the most powerful strongman in the area.[38]

The anti-Jan Mohammed factions throughout Uruzgan were soon looking for support and alliances and in many cases found them in the Taliban. Because of the conflict, hundreds of families left their districts for Kandahar and other locations, among them several tribal khans. Their departure allowed the influence of the Taliban to spread further. Once the Taliban had successfully penetrated the villages, they started their own purge of hostile elements, but more effectively than Jan Mohammed or his local allies.[39]

In Helmand the recruitment of locals in the Taliban's ranks was first reported in the summer of 2004. They recruited among communities that suffered harassment at the hands of police and security forces. During the first two to three years of the insurgency, Helmand was not particularly welcoming to the Taliban. In Musa Qala, for example, the Taliban first tried to establish a base in 2004, but did not find much local support and had to leave. By 2006, however, they had become very popular there. The Taliban attributed their success to the abuses of the governor, Sher Mohammed Akhundzada, and his militias, as well as to his refusal or inability to mend his ways or pay compensation despite the mediation of a tribal jirga. Like elsewhere, Karzai's cronies were antagonising many communities, throwing them into the arms of the Taliban. The insurgents did not have to do much, except approach the victims of the pro-Karzai strongmen and promise them protection and support. Attempts by local elders to seek protection in Kabul routinely ended nowhere as the wrongdoers enjoyed either direct US support or Karzai's sympathy. Dad Mohammed Khan, NSD chief of Helmand province, was particularly notorious for his abuses, but retained his position for a long time due to his direct connection with US forces, who thought he was serving them well. Only in 2006 was he removed at the insistence of UNAMA.[40]

A typical case concerned Ishaqzai communities, which had been very influential in Helmand under the Taliban regime, at the expense of the Alizais who had dominated the province until 1994. With the fall of the Taliban, Alizai circles around governor Sher Mohammed Akhundzada were once again elevated to the power they had been holding in 1981–94 and proceeded to marginalise and 'tax' Ishaqzai communities. In 2006 a violent conflict broke out. The Taliban exploited the conflict to consolidate their influence in Sangin district, where the Ishaqzai are the majority of the population, but this did not prevent them from maintaining their pockets of support among Alizai clans hostile to Sher Mohammed, such as in Baghran and in other parts of northern Helmand. Then, when the government and its international sponsors started a half-hearted attempt to eradicate the poppy fields in Helmand, support for the Taliban in the villages was immediately boosted. At that point any expression of support for the government in northern Helmand became impossible. Even the governor, a close ally of president Karzai, and his intelligence chief admitted to that. British troops reported that they could feel the hostility of the locals and that pro-Taliban tapes were openly sold in the bazaar. Stone-throwing by villagers at convoys of foreign troops was not unusual. Villagers appeared to act as informers of the Taliban and seemingly cooperated in setting up ambushes with them. The popularity of the Taliban was not limited to Musa Qala or Sangin. Even a district like Gereshk, not far from Lashkargah, was in 2006 fully infiltrated by the Taliban, who could be spotted in the roads of the district centre without the police daring to intervene. The countryside was *de facto* under Taliban control and even the district governor was admitting that the population was opposed to the government.[41]

The situation in the south was further complicated by the fact that in 2004–5, in part because of the pressure of the international community to clean up his act and in part due to the manipulations of local allies, Karzai and his circle started dropping their local allies one by one. As a result, the old jihadi strongmen stopped acting as a bulwark against the Taliban in 2004–5, as they were being marginalised.[42] This was the case for the Alkozai commander, Mullah Naqibullah, who gradually lost any influence over the provincial authorities and consequently the ability to reward and maintain the loyalty of large numbers of followers (see 1.2 *'Rebuilding' the Afghan state*). The number of Alkozais actively fighting in the insurgency remained relatively low, but the main impact seems to have been that the militarily powerful Alkozai militias were no longer committed to keeping the Taliban away from Kandahar. Because most of Kandahar's police was Alkozai, the development was bound to have a significant impact. The first Taliban teams were spotted in Alkozai-populated Arghandab in 2005, just after the loss of control of the police by the Alkozai. By 2006 the Taliban were talking of courting the sympathy of the population of Arghandab Valley of Kandahar province by mobilising them against the corrupt local police. Mullah Naqibullah continued to maintain his distance from both the government and the Taliban, at least in public: he complained about the behaviour of foreign troops, advocated talking to the insurgents but at the same time invited locals not to join the Taliban. Similarly, in Helmand after the demise of Governor Sher Mohammed Akhundzada in early 2006, his militias stopped actively pursuing the Taliban, allowing a rapid deterioration of security.[43]

c) *The east*

In the east, as in the south-east, the success of the Neo-Taliban was modest. This was due to several factors:

- like in the south-east, tribal structures maintained a high degree of cohesion and of ability to self-rule and self-govern;
- the Taliban always had weak roots in this area, hence the presence of few former members of the Movement to be recruited back into active warfare; Hizb-i Islami members were present in greater numbers, but had often re-integrated in society;
- the presence of a relatively strong intelligentsia, with at least some tribal connections;
- the presence of strong nationalist feelings, which played against an insurgency widely seen as a Pakistani stooge.

Nangarhar province, where all these elements of anti-insurgent resilience were present, proved the toughest nut to crack. An uneasy pro-Kabul alliance between the Arsalai family and warlord Hazrat Ali managed to maintain control over Nangarhar's tribes, combining long-established wealth, connections, influence, tribal management and newly acquired military strength. In Nangarhar educational levels are also significantly higher than the Afghan average. The Nangarhari intelligentsia seems to have maintained strong tribal connections and therefore some influence in the rural areas, correspondingly weakening the role of the clergy. Significantly, the only areas within Nangarhar that the insurgents managed to penetrate to any extent were Hisarak and the Khugyani districts, all characterised by lower educational levels and a greater strength of clerical networks. The comparatively dynamic economy of Nangarhar was more successful than that of other provinces in offering opportunities to the mostly educated cadres of Hizb-i Islami. Finally, Nangarhar is probably the province in Afghanistan where nationalist feelings run highest, due to the prevalence of tribes who live straddling the border with Pakistan and who suffered greatly in the past sixty years whenever Pakistan closed the border to put pressure on Kabul's government.[44]

Hizb-i Islami used to have influence in many villages along the Jalalabad–Torkham road, but it either did not succeed or did not try to reactivate military activities there, although there were allegations that the area was used for planning activities elsewhere. Opportunities were not missing for the Taliban and Hizb-i Islami: Nangarhar was the only province in Afghanistan where in 2005 poppy eradication was implemented effectively, due largely to the cooperation of the governor, Din Mohammed (a member of the Arsalai family). Then the farmers failed to receive the promised compensation, or received only a fraction of it. Rumours abounded of corruption. But the farmers did not turn to the Taliban in significant numbers. Even when Mawlawi Khalis, the old leader of a splinter group of Hizb-i Islami, sided with the insurgency in October 2003, it did not have any appreciable impact outside his home areas in the Khugyani districts. By 2006 some signs of a slow degradation of security in outlying districts were reported. For example, in a single week in the autumn of 2006 twenty-three security-related incidents were recorded in Nangarhar province. Relatively large groups of insurgents were also observed moving around the western districts, a fact which suggests at least some tolerance of their presence by local communities. By early 2007 the insurgents had started attacking local administrators in remote areas, according to a pattern already seen elsewhere. Some incidents related to the behaviour of US forces in the province, such as house searches without accompanying Afghan troops, the killing of a local cleric in a raid against alleged insurgents and the shooting of civilians following a suicide attack, are likely to have contributed to turning the mood of the population increasingly against the foreign troops. Despite all this, by early 2007 Nangarhar was still the most secure province among those bordering Pakistan.[45]

None of the other three eastern provinces was blessed by this combination of factors of resilience. In all three the economy was far from dynamic and former cadres of Hizb-i Islami faced much greater challenges to reintegrate in society. Both the intelligentsia and nationalist feelings were very weak if present at all, especially in Kunar and Nuristan. Although tribal structures were strong in Kunar and Nuristan, tribal governance was suffering the absence of big and established strongmen with good self-governance skills and the consequent political fragmentation. In these two provinces, therefore, government presence and influence was extremely weak, even in terms of alliances with local strongmen. By the 1990s these regions had been largely 'colonised' by Salafi preachers, who were also often organised politically and hostile to the central government. Due to this extreme weakness of the government, in Kunar, in Nuristan and in the northern districts of Laghman, in 2002–3 the insurgents were already able to operate there without much hindrance. Only in the Pashai fiefdom of Hazrat Ali (Nangarhar and Laghman) and in the heavily patrolled southern districts of Laghman was government presence able to keep the insurgents at bay.[46]

Although in Kunar the insurgents seem to have been successful in recruiting a fair number of local former mujahidin of the 1980s and in winning the tolerance or even the passive help of many villagers, they did not score great successes in allying with local communities. This was likely the result of a government presence so weak that it

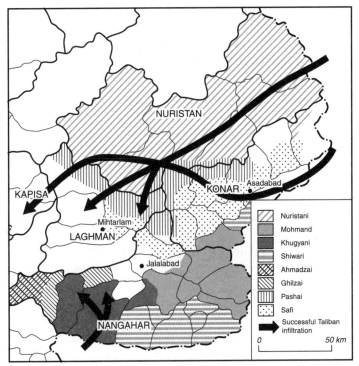

Map 5. Main tribes of eastern Afghanistan.
Source: interviews with local intellectuals and tribal notables, Jalalabad, February 2007.

was not even able to antagonise local communities, which in most cases appeared keen to maintain their autonomy *vis-à-vis* both insurgents and government. A rare exception was Koringal Valley in Pech district, where the local population had a strong tradition of hostility towards the central government. The locals were trying to protect their illegal timber trade from government regulation. The already difficult relationship of the government with the Koringalis was probably made worse by the attitude of district governors such as Mohammed Rehman, who first banned supplies of foods to the valley, then refused to issue identity cards to the valley's residents, and finally threatened to raise a tribal militia to invade the valley and punish the residents. Another area in which the presence of local insurgents had support among the population was Mail valley of Alisheng district (Laghman), where Commander Pashtun seems to have been a popular figure.[47]

d) *The rest of Afghanistan*

In the rest of Afghanistan recruitment among disenfranchised communities had achieved success in some isolated pockets of territory. In Bala-e Murghab and Ghormach of Baghdis, rivalries among local communities created an environment in which the Taliban managed to linger on after 2001, even if the distance from the Pakistan border made logistical support very difficult. During 2003–4 violent incidents in Baghdis were attributed to the Taliban by local authorities, although other sources described the attacks as the result of ethnic strife between the supporters of Governor Ismail Khan and some local Pashtun communities, or as inter-tribal clashes. Baghdis was also allegedly used by the Taliban to infiltrate neighbouring Faryab province. After a lull, in 2006 some insurgent activity was again reported in Baghdis. In northern Afghanistan NATO identified five areas of potential Taliban infiltration, even if there was little sign yet of this occurring.[48]

In Herat the conflict between several Pashtun communities and the Tajiks in control of the central government, as well as within Pashtun communities in Shindand and other districts, offered opportunities for the Taliban to infiltrate. After 2001 Ismail Khan, who had taken control of the western region, maintained only a precarious hold over the predominantly Pashtun districts of the west (Ghuryan, Kohsan and Gulran) and of the south (Adraskan, Shindand). His decision to keep Pashtuns out of positions of power and influence had been a major irritant to their communities, whose leaders also complained of Pashtun tribal leaders being assassinated, allegedly in an organised manner.[49] The abusive behaviour of Ismail Khan's militias against the local Pashtuns seems to have had a unifying effect on the tribes. In July 2002 a group of Pashtun tribal leaders gathered in Herat (presumably clandestinely) and prepared a petition to President Karzai, asking for the removal of Ismail Khan and for an enquiry into the abuses of his 'Tajik militias'. Soon Amanullah Khan, a strongman from Zeerkoh (Shindand), emerged to unify, in part, tribal opposition. Throughout 2002–4 Amanullah Khan survived all attempts by Ismail Khan to overcome him and even launched occasional counterattacks. His mere ability to survive politically and militarily turned out to be a winning card. He began to attract the support of disgruntled Pashtuns throughout the province and beyond. Hundreds of Pashtuns from Ghuryan and other districts joined his ranks. In Farah a former Taliban commander, Mullah Sultan, supported him. At the decisive moment he succeeded in mobilising support from as far afield as the southern provinces, obtaining the help of Gul Agha Shirzai and other strongmen, who sent hundreds of volunteers to fight in his ranks as well as money and weapons. By the summer of 2004 he was able to field a force of a few thousand motivated fighters, many of whom had suffered at the hands of Ismail Khan's men. With some support from Kabul, at least according to Ismail Khan, Amanullah Khan emerged as the leading player in an offensive organised with other disgruntled strongmen and warlords of the region, which in the summer of 2004 weakened Ismail Khan sufficiently for the central government to sack him from the position of governor of Herat. Following Ismail Khan's removal, tension and incidents continued in the region, as the anti-Ismail alliance proved unable to control the situation. The fact that there were no active remnants of the Taliban in the province until 2005 slowed the attempts of the insurgents to exploit the situation, but in that year the first reports of Taliban infiltration emerged with the capture of some emissaries in Herat city. Soon a terrorist campaign started in and around Herat. During 2006 the first manifestations of guerrilla activity emerged in Adraskan and Gulran districts, both populated by the most disenfranchised Pashtun communities. The alliance with Kabul of Amanullah Khan might have contributed to prevent the Taliban from infiltrating the countryside more effectively, but the killing of Amanullah in a tribal conflict in October 2006 removed the last barrier to Taliban penetration and the deteriorating security situation in the district forced the police to deploy new security

	Estimated by Western sources	Claimed by Taliban	Estimated by Afghan government	Author's estimate
Operating from Pakistan	3,000–4,000			5,500
Based in Afghanistan				
Kunar				*500*
Nangarhar				*100*
Laghman				*200*
Nuristan				*200*
Total east				1,000
Kapisa	*200*			*200*
Kabul				*200*
Wardak				*100*
Logar				*300*
Total Kabul region				800
Khost				*100*
Paktia				*400*
Paktika				*900*
Ghazni		*900*		*900*
Total south-east				2,300
Zabul	*1,000–1,200*		*1,700*	*1,200*
Helmand	*1,500–2,000*	*2,500*		*2,000*
Uruzgan	*2,500*			*2,500*
Kandahar	*600–700*			*1,000*
Total south	5,000–6,000	12,000–15,000		6,700
Farah				*300*
Herat				*100*
Baghdis				*100*
Ghor				*200*
Total west			700	700
Bamian				100
Total based in Afghanistan				11,500
TOTAL	7,000–10,000			17,000

Table 3. Estimates of the strength of the Taliban, 2006.
Sources: press report, UN sources, US military, NATO/ISAF

posts there. Open warfare reached Shindand in April 2007, when following the killing of an American soldier a major operation was mounted, leading to the killing of over a hundred Afghans, including many civilians. Judging from the subsequent wave of protest, it would appear that local opinion was turned decisively against the foreign troops as a result of the violence.[50]

North-east of Kabul the Taliban and Hizb-i Islami maintained strong support among the Pashtun communities of Kapisa and particularly Tagab district, where they represented most of the population there and were divided in rival communities as well as opposed to the Tajik communities of the neighbouring districts. Apart from an estimated two hundred local insurgents, the Taliban were reported to have built up their presence in the area during 2006 to up to five hundred fighters, prompting a NATO offensive to clear the area. Three training centres were found during the offensive, highlighting how the area had already been turned into a stronghold for the insurgency. After the offensive the insurgents withdrew to Kunar and Nuristan, waiting for opportunities to re-infiltrate. In April 2007 they were back in strength and attacked the district centre, blocking the highway for two hours.[51]

Based on the previous discussion of the presence of the Taliban inside Afghanistan, an estimate of their strength province by province is provided in Table 3.

2.7 CHANGES IN RECRUITMENT PATTERNS

As the conflict progressed, victims of abuses by both Afghan and foreign troops and of the side-effects of US reliance on air power began to represent another important source of recruits for the Taliban. They produced large numbers of displaced people, who in many cases sought refuge in camps around the provincial centres, or in Kandahar city itself, where they were often struggling to make a living. These internal refugee camps then turned into recruitment grounds for the insurgents. The Taliban even claimed that at one point the majority of their recruits belonged to this category, although this statement is likely to contain a fair dose of propaganda. However, probably the main boost to the Taliban came not from the bombardment *per se*, but from the revelation that not only the government was weak, but also the foreign contingents supporting it were stretched thin and had a limited capability to control the country. To Afghan villagers, the ability of NATO and the Coalition to win all battles brought little comfort, as the Taliban's ability to roam around in the villages was clearly not going to be challenged, nor their mountain strongholds eliminated. The expectation that the Taliban would eventually emerge as the winners of the conflict, or at least force for themselves a favourable compromise, also contributed to push villagers towards them. By the autumn of 2006 wild rumours were circulating among the population, concerning an impending national uprising, negotiations between the Taliban and other groups opposed to the Karzai administration, negotiations between the Americans and the Taliban, and so on. Even where the Taliban had little direct support, the unpopularity of the government and what was perceived as the 'disrespectful' behaviour of the foreign troops, fuelled by lack of understanding for the local culture, had the effect of dividing and demoralising the opposition to the insurgents and creating some nostalgia for the time when the Taliban were in power. A change in the mood of the population seems, for example, to have occurred in Kandahar during the summer of 2006. Taliban elements were openly circulating in the city, claiming to journalists that they were even able to introduce themselves as Taliban to fellow Kandaharis. The gathering of financial and logistical support in Kandahar allegedly accelerated greatly in 2006, with the cooperation of many traders and businessmen, presumably to ingratiate themselves with the potential winners of the conflict. The Taliban were also claiming that many government officials were now helping them with supplies and even offering transport services. While these claims might well have been exaggerated for propaganda purposes, independent observers also felt that the mood of the population of Kandahar city was shifting. By the beginning of 2007 Taliban teams were beginning to gun down policemen within the city itself, which might be an indication of an enhanced ability to infiltrate the city. Other cities of Afghanistan seemed to some extent affected by the change too. The change in the attitude of the population was not limited to the south, but was detected even in Kabul. Several Afghan MPs, mostly supporting Karzai, expressed to journalists in December 2006 their feelings that the country was again drifting towards a generalised jihad against the foreigners and even implied some sympathy for such a trend.[52]

By 2005 or at the latest by late 2006 the Taliban seemed convinced that the wind was definitely blowing in their favour, a fact which tallies with reports that they were intent on mobilising forces for stepping up military operations. Feeling more confident, the Taliban increasingly focused their efforts at trying to achieve a national mobilisation and trigger a wider jihad movement. This effort consisted of at least three main components. The first, as shown in the Introduction and in this chapter, was aimed at spreading their influence at the village level as wide as possible. The second saw for the first time the Taliban targeting the cities. In the autumn of 2006 reports emerged that the Taliban had launched a big recruitment drive involving even areas outside their control or influence, such as Lashkargah, Kandahar city and refugee camps in central Helmand. Already in 2005 reports emerged that the insurgents were even trying to recruit a more educated constituency, judging from a number of arrests at Khost University in 2005, including students accused of planning terrorist attacks, and in Kabul, including at least one student from Kabul University (Sharia Law). The attempted recruitment of doctors to serve as support staff was also reported.[53]

The third component of this effort targeted the old jihadi commanders, who had mostly been fighting against the Taliban up until 2001. Coalition sources believed that attempts to recruit local strongmen ideologically close to the Taliban cause were going on at least in Kunar as early as 2002, allegedly with the help of some cash. Three such figures, including a relatively prominent one—Emergency Loya Jirga delegate and leader of a Salafi group, Haji Ruhollah—were actually arrested as early as June 2002 on allegation of working with the Taliban, although many critical voices argued against this accusation and the arrest might well have been the result of another 'bad tip'. In late 2003 Mullah Omar was reported to have issued an appeal to independent warlords, militia commanders and strongmen to join the Taliban. Even if this was true, such efforts were quite marginal at that time, both in terms of results and in terms of energy invested in them. By contrast, reports in 2006 suggested that the Taliban had started approaching former jihadi commanders of the 1980s war on a much larger scale, even offering them large one-off payments and monthly contributions of US$500 for joining the insurgency. Although by the end of 2006 it was still too early to see whether these efforts would succeed, it was already obvious that they had created more than a ripple in the Afghan political scene (see 4.9 *Alliances*).[54]

By late 2006–early 2007 the Taliban seemed intent on capitalising on a certain shift of opinion in their favour by relaxing their ideological strictures. At least in some of the areas under their control, such as Musa Qala, they were no longer demanding that men grow a beard, keep their hair short or refrain from watching movies. This appears to have broadened their appeal, particularly in the towns. Taliban commanders were telling journalists that they were not going to impose their convictions so 'harshly' as when they had previously been in power.[55]

NOTES

1   Carlotta Gall and Eric Schmitt, 'Taliban step up Afghan bombings and suicide attacks', *New York Times*, 21 October 2005; 'Interview with President Bush', *CNN*, 20 September 2006; 'Canadian-led offensive may have killed 1,500 Taliban fighters', *CBC News*, 20 September 2006; personal communication with UN official, December 2006; Massoud Ansari, 'Taliban butcher turns baker to fill his men's stomachs for war', *Daily Telegraph*, 15 October 2006; Suzanna Koster, 'Taliban fighters talk tactics – while safe in Pakistan', *Christian Science Monitor*, 9 November 2006; Wright (2006a); Benjamin Sand, 'Afghanistan's Taleban insurgency fueled by drug, terrorist money', *VOA*, 22 August 2006; van der Schriek (2005); Syed Saleem Shahzad,

'Fighting talk from Osama and the Taliban', *Asia Times Online*, 25 April 2006; Robert Burns, 'Commander wants Afghan tours extended', *Associated Press*, 16 January 2007; David S. Cloud, 'U.S. says attacks are surging in Afghanistan', *New York Times*, 16 January 2007; M. Ilyas Khan, 'Taleban in Pakistan commend dead', *BBC News*, 12 January 2007; Riaz Khan and Matthew Pennington, 'Pride, grief and anger at a Taliban recruiting area in Pakistan', *Associated Press*, 28 January 2007; Marzban (2006).

2   David Wood, 'Afghan war needs troops', *Baltimore Sun*, 7 January 2007; 'Menace taliban dans le Sud', *AFP*, 20 February 2004.

3   <http://news.bbc.co.uk/2/shared/bsp/hi/pdfs/07_12_ 06AfghanistanWhereThingsStand.pdf>; <http://65.109.167.118/pipa/pdf/ jan06/Afghanistan_Jan06_quaire.pdf>.

4   Carlotta Gall, 'Peacekeeper commander mired in Afghan combat', *New York Times*, 15 October 2006; 'Macht Taliban in Uruzgan neemt toe', <http:// www.rtl.nl/(/actueel/rtlnieuws/)/components/actueel/rtlnieuws/2006/10_ oktober/23/binnenland/1023_0020_taliban_rukken_op.xml>; Karimi (2006), pp. 119–23 (courtesy of J. van den Zwan, Crisis States Research Centre, London); Paul McGeough, 'Winning hearts and minds is keeping the Taliban at bay', *Sydney Morning Herald*, 22 February 2007; Shahzad (2007), p. 7.

5   Syed Saleem Shahzad, 'Taliban's trail leads to Pakistan', *Asia Times Online*, 13 December 2001; Michael Ware, 'Encountering the Taliban', *Time*, 23 March 2002; Massoud Ansari, 'Almost two years after they were defeated, thousands join the Taliban's new jihad', *Telegraph*, 7 September 2003; Elizabeth Rubin, 'In the land of the Taliban', *New York Times Magazine*, 22 October 2006; Juliette Terzieff, 'Pakistani tribesmen stay fundamentally faithful to Taliban; Farmers put down plows to take up arms against U.S.', *San Francisco Chronicle*, 11 November 2003; Massoud Ansari, 'On the job with a Taliban recruiter', *Asia Times Online*, 27 November 2003; Wright (2006a); Jason Burke, 'Stronger and more deadly, the terror of the Taliban is back', *Observer*, 16 November 2003; Borhan Younus, 'Taliban hit and run, and come back for more', *Afghan Recovery Report*, no. 185 (10 September 2005); Wright (2006a); Phil Zabriskie and Steve Connors, 'Where are the Taliban now?', *Time*, 24 September 2002; Nivat (2006), pp. 80–93; interview with UN official, Herat, April 2004.

6   Interview with Massoud Kharokhel, 1 October 2006, Tribal Liaison Office, Kabul; Wright (2006a).

7   David Montero, 'Why the Taliban appeal to Pakistani youth', *Christian Science Monitor*, 16 June 2006; International Crisis Group (2006b), p. 22; Syed Saleem Shahzad, 'Revolution in the Pakistani mountains', *Asia Times Online*, 23 March 2006; interview with Abdul Rashid Waziri, former Minister of Tribal Affairs, Kabul, February 2007.

8   On this see Giustozzi (2006).

9   Personal communication with Massoud Karokhel, Tribal Liaison Office, Kabul, February 2007.

10 Benjamin Sand, 'Afghanistan's Taleban insurgency fueled by drug, terrorist money'; Rachel Morarjee, 'Taliban goes for cash over ideology', *Financial Times*, 25 July 2006; Declan Walsh, 'Kandahar under threat, war raging in two provinces and an isolated president. So what went wrong?', *Guardian*, 16 September 2006; Claudio Franco, 'In remote Afghan camp, Taliban explain how and why they fight', *San Francisco Chronicle*, 21 January 2007; Owais Tohid, 'Arid Afghan province proves fertile for Taliban', *Christian Science Monitor*, 14 July 2003; 'A geographical expression in search of a state', *The Economist*, 6 July 2006; Kate Clark, 'Cash rewards for Taliban fighters', *File On 4, BBC Radio 4*, 28 February 2006; Mike Collett-White, 'Les taliban ne manquent pas de recrues', *Reuters*, 23 August 2003; Anthony Loyd, 'It's dawn, and the shelling starts. Time to go into the Taleban maze', *The Times*, 14 February 2007.

11 Wright (2006a); Carlotta Gall, 'Taliban continue to sow fear', *New York Times*, 1 March 2006; personal communication with foreign diplomat, Kabul, March 2007.

12 Daniel Cooney, 'General: hard-hit Taliban recruiting kids', *Associated Press*, 24 July 2005; 'Taliban start recruiting fighters in Ghazni', *Pajhwok Afghan News*, 7 August 2006.

13 For the opinion of a CIA officer in this regard see David Rohde and James Risen, 'C.I.A. review highlights Afghan leader's woes', *New York Times*, 5 November 2006; see also Wright (2006a).

14 Graeme Smith, 'Doing it the Dutch way in Afghanistan', *Globe and Mail*, 2 December 2006; International Crisis Group (2006a); Talatbek Masadykov (UNAMA Kandahar), quoted in Graeme Smith, 'Inspiring tale of triumph over Taliban not all it seems', *Globe and Mail*, 23 September 2006; Hans de Vreij, 'Gevaren in Uruzgan nemen toe', *Radio Nederland*, 2 May 2006, <http://www.wereldomroep.nl/actua/nl/nederlandspolitiek/dedden060501>; Syed Saleem Shahzad, 'Afghanistan's highway to hell', *Asia Times Online*, 25 January 2007; Elizabeth Rubin, 'In the land of the Taliban'; Kate Clark, 'Cash rewards for Taliban fighters'.

15 Interviews with police officers and UN officials in Takhar and Kunduz, May 2006. See also for example Halima Kazem, 'U.S. thins Taliban's ranks, but their ideological grip remains strong', *Christian Science Monitor*, 18 September 2003.

16 A point made by Barnett Rubin in 'The forgotten war: Afghanistan', interview with Joanne J. Myers, Carnegie Council, 14 March 2006.

17 See Roy (2000), Dorronsoro (2000) and Roy (2002). One survey was carried out by CPAU in Wardak in 2006–7.

18 See Trives (2006) and also Dorronsoro (2000).

19 See Harpviken *et al.* (2002), pp. 7–8.

20 On this shift see Dorronsoro (2000), pp. 11–12.

21 Halima Kazem, 'U.S. thins Taliban's ranks, but their ideological grip remains strong'; Elizabeth Rubin, 'Taking the fight to the Taliban', *New York Times Magazine*, 29 October 2006; Eric Schmitt and David Rohde, 'Afghan rebels

widen attacks', *New York Times*, 1 August 2004; Trives (2006); interview with Afghan journalist returning from the south, Kabul, 9 October 2006; Elizabeth Rubin, 'In the land of the Taliban'; 'Afghan police raid religious institutions in southern Afghanistan', *RFE/RL*, 10 July 2006.

22 Trives (2006); Wahidullah Amani, 'Afghanistan: a long, bloody summer ahead', *Afghan Recovery Report*, no. 219 (15 June 2006); Chris Sands, 'Kabul clerics rally behind Taliban', *Toronto Star*, 22 May 2006; personal communication with police officer, Teluqan, May 2006; personal communication with UN official, Kabul, March 2007.

23 April Witt, 'Afghan political violence on the rise', *Washington Post*, 3 August 2003; 'Taliban targets Muslim clerics in Afghanistan', *CBC News*, 5 August 2003; Declan Walsh, 'Taliban assassins target the clerics faithful to Kabul', *Observer*, 27 August 2006; Wright (2006a); interview with Maulana Obeidullah of the Peace Strengthening Commission, Kandahar, 28 January 2006.

24 Johnson and Mason (2007), pp. 76–9; *Cheragh*, 3 April 2007; Harm Ede Botje, 'We zitten darr goed', *Vrij Nederland*, 6 January 2007 (courtesy of J. van den Zwan, Crisis States Research Centre, London).

25 Interview with security officer, Kandahar, January 2006; Rahimullah Yusufzai, quoted in 'Senate body for launching Pak-Afghan inter-parliaments dialogue', *PakTribune*, 15 December 2006; personal communications with UN officials, Kabul, May 2004 and October 2006; personal communication with Niamatullah Ibrahimi (Crisis States Research Centre), Kabul, October 2006; Syed Saleem Shahzad, 'Taliban line up the heavy artillery', *Asia Times Online*, 21 December 2006; personal communication with UN official, Kabul, May 2005; Elizabeth Rubin, 'In the land of the Taliban'; Syed Saleem Shahzad, 'How the Taliban keep their coffers full', *Asia Times Online*, 10 January 2007; Graeme Smith, 'The Taliban: knowing the enemy', *Globe and Mail*, 27 November 2006. On this topic see also Giustozzi (2006).

26 Wright (2006a); Graeme Smith, 'Taliban are snubbed in their hometown', *Globe and Mail*, 17 April 2006; Jason Burke, 'Stronger and more deadly, the terror of the Taliban is back'; Tim McGirk, 'The Taliban on the run', *Time*, 28 March 2005; interview with Mir Akbar, Tribal Liaison Office, Gardez, 11 October 2006; Trives (2006); interview with security officer, Kandahar, January 2006; Carlotta Gall, 'Taliban continue to sow fear'; Les Perreaux, 'NATO urges Afghans to vacate volatile Panjwaii district', *Canadian Press*, 31 August 2006; Andrew Maykuth, 'An Afghan rebuilding takes shape', *Philadelphia Inquirer*, 6 October 2003; 'Musa Qala braced for NATO assault', *Afghan Recovery Report*, no. 240 (6 February 2007); 'Elders from five provinces demand government to negotiate with the opposition', *Musharekat-e Milli*, 13 February 2007.

27 Syed Saleem Shahzad, 'Taliban deal lights a slow-burning fuse', *Asia Times Online*, 11 February 2006; Alastair Leithead, 'Can change in Afghan tactics bring peace?', *BBC News*, 17 October 2006; Syed Saleem Shahzad, 'Taliban line up the heavy artillery'; 'Civilian casualties trigger anti-govt sentiments',

Pajhwok Afghan News, 21 August 2006; Danish Karokhel, 'Provincial election trouble', *Afghan Recovery Report*, no. 90 (22 December 2003).

28 'Afghanistan: un responsable tribal pendu par des talibans', *Xinhuanet*, 16 July 2005; UNAMA source, 1 October 2006; Elizabeth Rubin, 'In the land of the Taliban'; Les Perreaux, 'NATO urges Afghans to vacate volatile Panjwaii district'; Carlotta Gall, 'Taliban surges as U.S. shifts some tasks to NATO', *New York Times*, 11 June 2006; Françoise Chipaux, 'Les talibans font régner leur loi dans les provinces pachtounes du Sud', *Le Monde*, 7 October 2004; Pamela Constable, 'A NATO bid to regain Afghans' trust', *Washington Post*, 27 November 2006; Brian Hutchinson, 'First foray into Taliban area', *National Post*, 21 December 2006; Paul Watson, 'On the trail of the Taliban's support', *Los Angeles Times*, 24 December 2006; Richard Foot, 'Canada relying on Afghan police in Taliban offensive', *CanWest News Service*, 13 January 2007.

29 Cordesman (2007); Declan Walsh, 'Better paid, better armed, better connected – Taliban rise again', *Guardian*, 16 September 2006.

30 'A geographical expression in search of a state', *The Economist*, 6 July 2006; interview with UNAMA official, October 2006, Gardez; Philip G. Smucker, 'Afghanistan's eastern front', *U.S. News & World Report*, 9 April 2007.

31 Interview with Massoud Kharokhel, 1 October 2006, Tribal Liaison Office, Kabul; interview with Tribal Liaison Office official in Gardez, October 2006. See Trives (2006a) for more details on the insurgency in the southeast up to 2005; 'Sud-est de l'Afghanistan: "Ici, c'est la guerre!"', *AFP*, 20 September 2003; interview with UN official, Gardez, October 2006; Sara Daniel, 'Afghanistan: "Résister aux talibans? A quoi bon!"', *Le Nouvel Observateur*, 10 August 2006; 'Taliban start recruiting fighters in Ghazni', *Pajhwok Afghan News*, 7 August 2006; Mirwais Atal, 'US hearts and minds cash goes to Taliban', *Afghan Recovery Report*, 29 November 2006.

32 Antonio Giustozzi (forthcoming); interview with Afghan security officer, Kandahar, January 2006; Declan Walsh, 'Special deals and raw recruits employed to halt the Taliban in embattled Helmand', *Guardian*, 4 January 2007; David Rohde, 'G.I.s in Afghanistan on hunt, but now for hearts and minds', *New York Times*, 30 March 2004; Carsten Stormer, 'Winning hearts, minds and firefights in Uruzgan', *Asia Times Online*, 6 August 2004; Sara Daniel, 'Afghanistan: "Résister aux talibans? A quoi bon!"'.

33 On the Achakzai militias see Giustozzi (2006).

34 Adrien Jaulmes, 'Les forces spéciales françaises en Afghanistan face aux talibans', *Le Figaro*, 28 June 2006; interview with former Emergency Loya Jirga delegate from Farah, Kandahar, 26 January 2006; Elizabeth Rubin, 'In the land of the Taliban'; Graeme Smith, 'Inspiring tale of triumph over Taliban not all it seems'; Wright (2006a).

35 Owais Tohid, 'Arid Afghan province proves fertile for Taliban'; Elizabeth Rubin, 'Taking the fight to the Taliban'; Mohammed Weekh, 'Provincial tensions ahead of Loya Jirga', *Afghan Recovery Report*, no. 6 (28 May 2002); Françoise Chipaux, 'Dans le plus complet dénuement, la province afghane

de Zabul mène la lutte contre les talibans', *Le Monde*, 24 December 2003.

36 Griff Witte, 'Afghan province's problems underline challenge for U.S.', *Washington Post*, 30 January 2006; Karimi (2006), pp. 119–23 (courtesy of J. van den Zwan, Crisis States Research Centre, London); Harm Ede Botje, 'We zitten darr goed'; interview with tribal notable from Gezab, Kandahar, January 2006.

37 Interview with tribal notable from Gezab, Kandahar, January 2006; interview with tribal notable from Chora, April 2007.

38 Sayed Salahuddin and Mohammed Ismail Sameen, 'Afghan violence erupts, killing at least 61', *Reuters*, 13 August 2003; Afghan Independent Human Rights Commission (2004), pp. 21–2; Graeme Smith, 'Doing it the Dutch way in Afghanistan'; Joeri Boom, 'Tulbanden en Friese vlaggen', *De Groene Amsterdammer*, 12 May 2006; personal communication with foreign diplomat, Kabul, February 2007.

39 See Saeed Zabuli, 'Taliban executes tribal elder in Daikundi', *Pajhwok Afghan News*, 25 December 2006, for the case of an elder hanged by the Taliban for supporting the government.

40 Eric Schmitt and David Rohde, 'Afghan rebels widen attacks'; Syed Saleem Shahzad, 'Rough justice and blooming poppies', *Asia Times Online*, 7 December 2006; Elizabeth Rubin, 'In the land of the Taliban'.

41 Rahmani (2006b); Alastair Leithead, 'Unravelling the Helmand impasse', *BBC News*, 21 December 2006; Syed Saleem Shahzad, 'Taliban line up the heavy artillery'; Carlotta Gall, 'Despite Afghan strictures, the poppy flourishes', *New York Times*, 16 February 2006; Eric Schmitt and David Rohde, 'Afghan rebels widen attacks'; Thomas Coghlan and Justin Huggler, 'A ruthless enemy, a hostile population and 50C heat', *Independent*, 9 July 2006; Raymond Whitaker, 'Blood and guts: at the front with the poor bloody infantry', *Independent*, 1 October 2006; Christina Lamb, 'Have you ever used a pistol?', *Sunday Times*, 2 July 2006; Eric de Lavarène, 'La province de tous les dangers', *RFI*, 19 March 2006.

42 For more details see Giustozzi (forthcoming).

43 Interview with Afghan security officer, Kandahar, January 2006; personal communication with Farouq Azam, London, January 2006; personal communication with UN official, Kandahar, January 2006; see also Graeme Smith, 'The Taliban: knowing the enemy'; Carlotta Gall, 'NATO's Afghan struggle: build, and fight Taliban', *New York Times*, 13 January 2007; Murray Brewster, 'Influential warlord urges Afghan youths to lay down arms, reject Taliban', *Canadian Press*, 24 January 2007; interview with Afghan security officer, Kandahar, January 2006.

44 Interviews with members of the Afghan intelligentsia, Nangarhar University and Pedagogical Institute of Jalalabad, February 2007; interview with the Chief of Police of Nangarhar, February 2007; interview with Afghan journalists, Jalalabad, February 2007.

45 Syed Saleem Shahzad, 'Taliban raise the stakes in Afghanistan', *Asia Times Online*, 30 October 2003; Christian Parenti, 'Taliban rising', *Nation*

Magazine, 12 October 2006; Rahimullah Yusufzai, 'Khalis declares jihad against US', *The News*, 29 October 2003; Senlis Council (2006d), p. 27; 'Afghan district chief escapes assassination attempt', *AFP*, 18 January 2007; 'Nangarhar council on strike over killing', *AFP*, 7 February 2007.

46 Interview with UN official, Jalalabad, February 2006.

47 Personal communication with Massoud Karokhel, Tribal Liaison Office, Kabul, February 2007; Declan Walsh, 'In the heartland of a mysterious enemy, US troops battle to survive', *Guardian*, 5 December 2006; personal communication with UN official, Jalalabad, February 2007; interview with BBC journalist Khpolwak Sapai, Kabul, 5 March 2007.

48 'Seven killed in Afghanistan "Taliban" battle', *AFP*, 26 March 2003; personal communication with UN official, Herat, April 2004; Senlis Council (2006a), ch. 1, p. 61; personal communication with UN official, Maimana, November 2004; 'NATO watchful of Taliban in northern Afghanistan', *AFP*, 20 April 2007.

49 For the case of Yunis Khan in Herat see 'Afghan faction says Herat ruler killed tribal chief', *Reuters*, 4 November 2002. Arbab Nasar was another Pashtun tribal leader assassinated in Ghuryan (interview with former militia commander and tribal notable, Herat, September 2005).

50 *AFP*, 26 July 2002; Interview with former district official and teacher from Shindand, Herat 26 September 2005; Amy Waldman, 'Strife exposes deep and wide ethnic tensions', *New York Times*, 6 September 2004; Anthony Loyd, 'Afghan warlord closes in on prize city', *The Times*, 25 August 2004; personal communication with Herati politician, Herat, October 2006; Ahmad Quraishi, 'Three policemen among four killed in Herat', *Pajhwok Afghan News*, 27 December 2006; *Sada-ye Jawan Radio*, Herat, in Dari 1230 gmt 14 October 2006; Rachel Morarjee, 'Afghan clashes raise concerns', *Financial Times*, 3 May 2007; 'No probe of reported civilian deaths in Afghanistan: US military', *AFP*, 2 May 2007.

51 Jason Motlagh, 'Taming the Afghan badlands', *UPI*, 29 September 2006; 'Operation helps curb Taliban attacks', *Associated Press*, 21 December 2006; Anna K. Perry, 'Operation Al Hasn brings hope to Tagab valley', *Freedom Watch*, 20 November 2006, <www.cfc-a.centcom.mil/ Freedom%20Watch/2006/11-November/20nov06.pdf>; Syed Saleem Shahzad, 'Afghanistan's highway to hell'; 'Heavy fighting erupts northeast of Afghan capital', *Reuters*, 17 April 2007; personal communication with military attaché, Kabul, April 2007; *Cheragh*, 19 April 2007.

52 Renata D'Aliesio, 'Hundreds of Taliban die in battle for their training school', *Calgary Herald*, 2 October 2006; Wright (2006a); Senlis Council (2006b), ch. 4; Kathy Gannon, 'Taliban comeback traced to corruption', *Associated Press*, 24 November 2006; 'Civilian casualties trigger anti-govt sentiments', *Pajhwok Afghan News*, 21 August 2006; interview with Afghan journalist returning from the south, Kabul, October 2006; David Rohde and James Risen, 'C.I.A. review highlights Afghan leader's woes'; personal communications with Afghan MPs, tribal leader and notables, Kabul and

Gardez, October 2006; Carsten Stormer, 'Winning hearts, minds and firefights in Uruzgan'; Syed Saleem Shahzad, 'How the Taliban prepare for battle', *Asia Times Online*, 5 December 2006; Pamela Constable, 'Afghan city's rebound cut short. Battles between NATO forces, resurgent Taliban make ghost town of Kandahar', *Washington Post*, 19 August 2006; 'In Kandahar, the Taliban are not a bad memory', *AFP*, 8 December 2006; Ahmad Farzan, 'Two police officers gunned down in Kandahar', *Pajhwok Afghan News*, 26 January 2007; Chris Sands, 'Afghan MPs predict very big war', *Dominion*, 19 December 2006; Jean MacKenzie, 'Bring back the Taleban', Afghan Blog, <http://www.iwpr.net/?o=f-328686&o1=month-2,year-2007&apc_state=hendarr>, 22 January 2007.

53 Syed Saleem Shahzad, 'How the Taliban prepare for battle'; Syed Saleem Shahzad, 'The vultures are circling', *Asia Times Online*, 13 December 2006; Senlis Council (2006b), ch. 4, pp. 13–14; Scott Baldauf and Ashraf Khan, 'New guns, new drive for Taliban', *Christian Science Monitor*, 26 September 2005; Rahmani (2006a).

54 Davis (2002); UNHCR, 'Chronology of Events in Afghanistan', September 2002, p. 3; Pepe Escobar, 'The roving eye part 1: exit Osama, enter Hekmatyar', *Asia Times Online*, 9 October 2002; Jason Burke, 'Stronger and more deadly, the terror of the Taliban is back'; Senlis Council (2006a), p. 18.

55 'Living under the Taleban', *Afghan Recovery Report* (IWPR), no. 249 (4 April 2007); David Loyn, 'On the road with the Taliban', *BBC News*, 21 October 2006.

3

ORGANISATION OF THE TALIBAN

The jihad of the 1980s and early 1990s was characterised by a division into a multitude of political parties and groups, of which fifteen were recognised by either Pakistan or Iran. Moreover, the majority of these parties exercised no real control over the armed groups affiliated to them inside Afghanistan. The result was a chaotic jihad with no overall strategy, unity or even coordination, prisoner of the segmentarity of Afghan society. This begs the question of how cohesive the Neo-Taliban and their new jihad movement are. There are obviously disparate groups and components fighting within the insurgency, but there is no consensus on how this affects its cohesiveness. One line of thinking is that because of a lack of 'coherence and cohesion among the different groups ... internal contradictions will likely increase'.[1]

In the early years of the insurgency, the Neo-Taliban did experience a split. Jaish-ul Muslimeen (Army of Muslims) quit the Taliban in September 2003, allegedly over a controversy concerning the need to intensify the insurgency. Led by a Kandahari commander Sayd Akbar Agha, it styled itself after the mainstream Taliban, even appointing a ten-member council as leadership. Mullah Ishaq, deputy military commander of the Taliban in the southern region, was appointed as military commander of the new group. At that time the group claimed to control a third of the Taliban's fighting force, particularly in Zabul and Helmand, where some local commanders had been critical of Mullah Omar's leadership. Whatever its initial success, between the second half of 2004 and the first half of 2005 the Jaish started to rapidly lose support, with its commanders turning back to the mainstream Taliban. By June 2005, when the group merged back into the Taliban, the leadership of the Jaish claimed much more modestly to have 750 fighters. Pakistani sources close to the Taliban expressed the feeling that the Jaish was an attempt by Pakistanis to create a more pliable insurgent movement, which would be more amenable to a political deal once the time was ripe. The fact that the leader of the group, Akbar Agha, was arrested by Pakistan in December 2004 together with another seventeen alleged Taliban middle rank members diminishes the credibility of this interpretation, although his involvement in the kidnapping of three UN workers in 2004 and his rift with other leaders of the group over the alleged US$1.5 million ransom might also be a reason for his elimination from the scene.[2]

The fate of the Jaish suggests that despite the lack of a sophisticated structure of command and control (there is, for example, no report of the existence of anything resembling 'political commissars'), the Neo-Taliban maintained a strong cohesiveness. Another, earlier and allegedly Pakistani-sponsored attempt to promote a group of Taliban independent of Mullah Omar and his circle had fared no better. The son of Nabi Mohammed, the old leader of Harakat-e Enqelab, a party which had once included most of the first generation of Taliban, was apparently involved in the effort to form a party of moderate Taliban, ready to sign a political deal with Kabul. Jamiat-i Khudam-ul Koran was launched in early 2002 by a group of former officials of the Taliban regime and initially attracted a significant number of supporters, but it was largely reabsorbed into the mainstream Taliban within a couple of years. It is not even entirely clear whether Jami'at-i Khudam-ul Koran was a genuinely separate group or just a front of the Taliban, as its members had mostly refused to condemn either Mullah Omar or Osama bin Laden until the very end of 2001. In 2004, when its leader Mohammed Amin Mojaddedi travelled to Kabul to register the group for the parliamentary elections, the rest of the party did not follow. In more recent years local non-state armed groups surfaced, particularly in the south, which do

similar problems surfaced, and again in 2007. In Uruzgan, the wheat seeds sent by the Americans to be distributed to the farmers as an alternative to the poppies were sold by government officials rather than distributed to the farmers. There are clear signs that the Taliban did not hesitate to exploit this opportunity, despite their earlier opposition to the growing of poppies (2000–1). In Helmand they appear to have offered protection to the farmers targeted by eradication. Certainly the poppy harvest area started growing exponentially after the Taliban firmly established themselves in the province. UNODC estimated that during 2006 the harvested area grew by 250 per cent, while in early 2007 local authorities estimated a near doubling of the area under cultivation over 2006. In Kandahar, they were even reported to have offered financial assistance to farmers whose fields were being eradicated, in exchange for support in fighting against the government. The decision in late 2006 not to pay compensation to farmers any more for the eradication of their fields is also unlikely to have been welcomed. This, however, fits into a more general pattern of the Taliban exploiting any differences between local communities and central government (see 2.6 *Recruiting local communities*) and should not be construed to imply necessarily that the Taliban were specifically targeting poppy-growing communities for support. In any case, once the Taliban established themselves in poppy-growing areas, they did cooperate with both poppy-growing farmers and the traffickers. Despite the Taliban's claims that they only support the farmers but not the traffickers, there is evidence that apart from taxing the poppy harvest, the Taliban might sometimes have provided protection to drug convoys. It is not clear, however, whether this happened in exchange for cash or whether it was an 'exchange of favours', such as the provision of shelter and food. Clearly the traffickers enjoy safe passage in Taliban-controlled areas. It is also believed that on some occasions traffickers' militias and Taliban have fought together against the intrusion of foreign forces in the strongholds. Drug traffickers might be helping the Taliban in order to create a situation of insecurity which makes poppy eradication and more general counter-narcotics impractical. Some sources even suggest that the relationship between the traffickers and growers and the Taliban might with time have become more organic and have ended in marriage alliances, in line with Taliban practice in dealing with local communities.[7]

Does this evidence amount to a proof that the insurgency is funded by drug revenue? A more accurate analysis suggests that such a claim is somewhat off the mark. Much of what is described as the Taliban's cosiness with traffickers and growers reflects the Movement's readiness to exploit any opportunity offered by free trade (see 1.1 *The 'Ideology' of the Taliban* and 2.2 *Early recruitment*). This is, for example, the case when donkeys transporting drugs out of Afghanistan are used to take weapons and ammunition to Afghanistan for the Taliban, as suggested in some reports. How important the revenue from the narcotics trade is to the Taliban is not clear. Some Afghan and international officials suggest that the Taliban make more money than other external partners involved in the trade, such as government functionaries. Others, including most foreign diplomats, maintain that drugs remain a secondary source of revenue for the Taliban and that there is little evidence of them encouraging the farmers to grow poppies and of their involvement in the trade. This author tends to side with the second group, for three reasons. First, the traffickers are unlikely to be willing to give up a major share of their profits to the Taliban, particularly in the presence of overproduction and of competition from corrupt police officers and increasingly even ANA officers in courting their favours (see 6.3 *Afghan police* and 6.4 *Afghan National Army*).[8] Second, if substantial amounts of money were turned to field commanders, this would likely have resulted in a fragmentation of the Taliban chain of command, as commanders would become more autonomous. There is, however, no sign of that (see 3.1 *Cohesiveness of the Taliban*). To the extent that traffickers pay money to the insurgents, they are more likely to hand it over to field commanders, both because they are probably more approachable and because the traffickers have no interest in strengthening the leadership of a movement which might one day turn against them, as it did already in 2000. Third and last, the Taliban do not really control Afghanistan's borders and, as claimed by US and NATO sources, have to cross it in small groups or even as individuals (see 4.1 *Infiltration*). Therefore, it is not clear to what extent they would be of much help to traffickers in crossing the border with Pakistan, compared to the help which would derive from purchasing the collaboration of Afghanistan's border police and other security forces.

The issue of external sources of funding is for obvious reasons a difficult one to address. The Taliban have no qualms in admitting that they receive money from Arab sympathisers, while at the same time claiming that such financial support is not sufficient to acquire sophisticated anti-aircraft and other weaponry. Pakistani Islamic parties and groups like Jamaat-i Islami and Jamaat-ul Ulema are very vocal supporters of the Taliban insurgency and rank-and-file Taliban have admitted to journalists to have in the past received direct support from them, even if the Pakistan government has banned raising funds for jihadi activities.[9] As mentioned earlier, the question of whether the Pakistani authorities provide material help remains open (see 1.3 *The role of Pakistan*). What matters most from our perspective, however, is how external funding is channelled to the Taliban. Although no information is available in this regard, the fact that such disparate sources of funding did not lead to the permanent splitting of the Movement suggests that support must be channelled directly to the top leadership. How this can happen when jihadist movements worldwide have the tendency to be very fragmented organisationally is not clear, unless the Pakistani authorities imposed a degree of control over revenue as a pre-condition for letting the Taliban operate from their country and then channel it directly to the top leaders.

3.3 COMMAND STRUCTURE

The organisational structures of the Movement of the Taliban were far from very sophisticated. The function of political direction belonged to supreme leader Mullah Omar and to a leadership council (Rahbari Shura), appointed by Mullah Omar in March 2003 and composed initially of ten members but later expanded to twelve, then eighteen and finally to thirty-three (see Table 2 for the membership of the Rahbari Shura when it counted ten and twelve members [2003–4]). The expansion of the Shura reflected the need to balance its composition as the Movement expanded and tried to attract support throughout an ever greater part of Afghanistan. In addition to the Rahbari Shura, the Taliban seem to have established also a sort of Shadow Cabinet, with positions such as 'defence minister' (Haji Obeidullah) and 'minister responsible for religious questions' (Mullah Abdul Ali), but little information is available about the workings of this 'cabinet'. By the time the Rahbari Shura had expanded to twelve members, there had already been changes in its composition, possibly because of the changing correlation of forces within the Movement, but also because of combat losses. The most important development was the removal of Saifullah Mansoor (see 3.1 *Cohesiveness of the Taliban*). In October 2006 the formation of another council (Majlis al-Shura) was announced by Mullah Omar, but little was known of its functions except that it was composed of thirteen members, mostly well known commanders already members of the Rahbari Shura.[10]

The Taliban's military organisation was based on five operational zones (see Map 6), each led by an old guard Taliban commander (see Table 4). Two more commanders were in charge of the logistical areas of Quetta and Peshawar. The regional military command structure also saw many changes. In September 2003, a few months after its establishment, it was already necessary to replace Hafiz Abdur Rahim, military commander of the southern zone, killed in combat. Dangar was assassinated in November 2004 in Pakistan, but it is not clear who replaced him in the Kabul region. The largest of these regions, the south, appears to have been run initially by a triumvirate composed of Dadullah, Abdur Razzaq Akhund and Osmani, but Hafiz Abdur Rahman seems to have taken over at some point in

2003, until he was killed. Razzaq disappeared from the scene after allegedly developing some problems with the leadership on 'organisational and procedural matters', while Osmani and Dadullah did not get along well. As a result, when Dadullah was reappointed in 2004, Osmani apparently switched the military role with that of 'facilitator' in developing alliances with the southern tribes. According to Taliban sources there were headquarters in Baghran from where operations in the south were run, which did not play much of a role in the war up to early 2007, but was supposed to become of key importance once the 'final offensive' started. The most significant development appears to have been the appointment of Haqqani as overall military commander in 2006, a role earlier played somehow by the badly matched Dadullah/Osmani couple. The appointment seemed to have stemmed from Mullah Omar's dissatisfaction with the military performance of the southern fighters, which Haqqani, the most experienced of the Taliban commanders in terms of guerrilla operations, was supposed to improve. Haqqani had previously been in charge of military operations in the south-east. Although sources in NATO sometimes see Haqqani as the leader of a separate insurgency element, most sources agree that he remained loyal to Mullah Omar even if the relationship between the two went through a period of crisis in the last few years of the Taliban regime.[11]

Below the regional commanders the Taliban command structure included provincial and district commanders. The latter might have been appointed only in mid-2005, when Mullah Dadullah announced the establishment of provincial leadership councils. At the lowest level were tactical commanders, leading groups and teams of five to fifty men. There was not much formal organisation, but a considerable degree of flexibility in the number of men each commander was allowed to have, another 'free market' attitude aimed at maximising the incentives for local recruitment and motivating the commanders. However, a number of measures were taken to guarantee a minimal degree of discipline and balance. The rotation of commanders at the various levels seems to have been frequent and might

Military commanders	2003	2006
Kabul region	Anwar Dangar	?
East	Mullah Kabir	Mullah Kabir
South-east	Mullah Saifullah Mansoor	Sirajuddin Haqqani
South	Hafiz Abdur Rahim? Or Dadullah Razzaq and Osmani jointly	Mullah Dadullah
General commander	Baradar	Jalaluddin Haqqani

Table 4. Military leadership of the Taliban, 2003
Sources: press reports, interviews with locals in Kandahar.

Map 6. The Taliban's military commands.
Sources: press reports.

have been a deliberate attempt to maintain control and prevent the development of personal fiefdoms. The insistence on forming mixed groups of combatants, including mixing people from different tribes and provinces with the locals, might in part too have answered a similar concern. According to the Layeha of the Taliban, commanders were not allowed to take in fighters from other groups, a measure

92

presumably aimed both at preventing rifts among commanders and at preventing the emergence of big commanders who could turn into semi-independent warlords. In the end, much rested on the appointment of trusted and ideologically committed field commanders, even more than it would to most guerrilla movements. Although sometimes direct orders to mount operations were received, most of the time the local commanders acted autonomously, based on their understanding of the strategic and political aims of the Movement. Commitment was privileged over skills and often madrasa-educated young men wielded an unusual amount of power by the standards of a society like Afghanistan's, where age and experience are considered to be major sources of social status. Tactical mistakes were often forgiven as long as ideological purity was demonstrated. This was due to the difficulty of carrying out command and control from the top most of the time. The use of satellite phones as a means of strategic coordination and operational control of the insurgency had to be abandoned relatively early in the conflict, due to US monitoring of communications (see also 5.1 *Military technology of the insurgency*). It was replaced by old fashioned messengers, of course a much slower (but secure) system.[12]

NOTES

1 International Crisis Group (2006a), p. 8.
2 Syed Saleem Shahzad, 'Pakistan reaches into Afghanistan', *Asia Times Online*, 3 October 2006; Janullah Hashemzada, 'Jaishul Muslimeen returns to Taliban fold', *Pajhwok Afghan News*, 23 June 2005; Syed Saleem Shahzad, 'Another Taliban song and dance', *Asia Times Online*, 10 September 2004; Tim McGirk, 'The Taliban on the run', *Time*, 28 March 2005; 'Afghan hostage-takers disband after ransom dispute', *AFP*, 1 December 2004; 'Pak arrests UN workers' abductor', *PTI*, 11 December 2004.
3 Syed Saleem Shahzad, 'Time to talk: US engages the Taliban', *Asia Times Online*, 24 November 2005; Syed Saleem Shahzad, 'Taliban's trail leads to Pakistan', *Asia Times Online*, 13 December 2001; *Afghan Islamic Press*, Peshawar, in Pashto, 1621 gmt 9 June 2004; Syed Saleem Shahzad, 'Pakistan reaches into Afghanistan'; interview with former mujahidin commander from Ghazni, Kabul, October 2006.

4   Cordesman (2007); interview with Farouq Azam, London, January 2006; Syed Saleem Shahzad, 'Taliban's new commander ready for a fight', *Asia Times Online*, 23 May 2006; Graeme Smith, 'The Taliban: knowing the enemy', *Globe and Mail*, 27 November 2006; 'Afghanistan: captured spokesman reveals rifts within Taliban', *ADN Kronos*, 19 January 2007; 'Deep differences between Taliban leaders', *Anis*, 25 December 2006.

5   Sami Yousafzai and Urs Gehriger, 'A new layeha for the Mujahideen', *Die Weltwoche*, 29 November 2006, <http://www.signandsight.com/features/1071.html>; Christopher Dickey, 'Afghanistan: the Taliban's book of rules', *Newsweek*, 12 December 2006.

6   Elizabeth Rubin, 'In the land of the Taliban', *New York Times Magazine*, 22 October 2006; Syed Saleem Shahzad, 'How the Taliban keep their coffers full', *Asia Times Online*, 10 January 2007; Graeme Smith, 'Inspiring tale of triumph over Taliban not all it seems', *Globe and Mail*, 23 September 2006; Syed Saleem Shahzad, 'How the Taliban prepare for battle', *Asia Times Online*, 5 December 2006; Peter Bergen, 'Afghanistan 2007: problems, opportunities and possible solutions, testimony to the House Committee on Foreign Affairs', 15 February 2007.

7   Raymond Whitaker, 'Opium war revealed: major new offensive in Afghanistan', *Independent*, 21 January 2007; Griff Witte, 'Afghan province's problems underline challenge for U.S. resilient insurgency', *Washington Post*, 30 January 2006; Wright (2006b); Senlis Council (2006d), p. 21; Syed Saleem Shahzad, 'Afghanistan's highway to hell', *Asia Times Online*, 25 January 2007; 'Helmand heads for record poppy harvest', *Afghan Recovery Report*, no. 241 (9 February 2007); Tom Coghlan, 'Bribery wrecks drive to root out opium', *Daily Telegraph*, 27 February 2007.

8   Wright (2006b); Declan Walsh, 'Better paid, better armed, better connected —Taliban rise again', *Guardian*, 16 September 2006; Alastair Leithead, 'Unravelling the Helmand impasse', *BBC News*, 21 December 2006; Jelsma *et al.* (2006), p. 7.

9   'Menace taliban dans le Sud', *AFP*, 20 February 2004; Scott Baldauf and Owais Tohid, 'Taliban appears to be regrouped and well-funded', *Christian Science Monitor*, 8 May 2003.

10 'Jalaluddine Haqqani: une légende moudjahidine devenue figure des talibans', *AFP*, 20 February 2004; Sami Yousafzai and Urs Gehriger, 'A new layeha for the Mujahideen'; 'Mullah Omar names a new Majlis Shura', *MEMRI Special Dispatch Series*, no. 1310 (5 October 2006), <http://memri.org/bin/articles.cgi?Page=subjects&Area=jihad&ID=SP131006>.

11 *Reuters*, 17 March 2004; 'Afghan commander shot dead in Pakistan', *BBC Monitoring International Reports*, 12 November 2004; Rahimullah Yusufzai, 'Pakistan: Taliban chief forms body to organize jihad against foreign troops', *The News*, 24 June 2003; Paul Watson, 'Widespread U.S. intelligence leaks in Afghanistan', *Los Angeles Times*, 12 April 2006; Syed Saleem Shahzad, 'Taliban line up the heavy artillery', *Asia Times Online*, 21 December 2006; 'Taliban military commander Mullah Dadallah: we are in contact with Iraqi

mujahideen, Osama bin Laden and Al-Zawahiri', *MEMRI Special Dispatch Series*, no. 1180 (2 June 2006); Syed Saleem Shahzad, 'Taliban's new commander ready for a fight'; Cordesman (2007); 'Jalaluddine Haqqani: une légende moudjahidine devenue figure des talibans', *AFP*, 20 February 2004.
12 Schiewek (2006), pp. 158-9; interview with Afghan security officer, Kandahar, January 2006; Sami Yousafzai and Urs Gehriger, 'A new layeha for the Mujahideen'; Christopher Dickey, 'Afghanistan: the Taliban's book of rules'; Syed Saleem Shahzad, 'Time out from a siege', *Asia Times Online*, 9 December 2006; Syed Saleem Shahzad, 'Taliban line up the heavy artillery'; Syed Saleem Shahzad, 'Another Taliban song and dance'.

4

THE TALIBAN'S STRATEGY

Chapters 2 and 3 explained how the core group of Taliban which started the insurgency in 2002 was relatively successful in recruiting a large following and in maintaining a sufficient degree of cohesiveness. Their next task towards mounting a significant challenge to Kabul was to produce a well crafted strategy and implement it effectively. This had to be done from scratch since the Taliban had little experience in fighting an insurgency. The main exception was Jalaluddin Haqqani, but initially his role was limited to the south-east. Allies like Hizb-i Islami never cooperated closely with the Neo-Taliban at the top level (see 4.9 *Alliances*). Whether the rigidity of the Taliban's leadership is interpreted as a principled stand or as mere stupidity, the intellectual resources and flexibility to conceive a fully-fledged strategy were clearly absent.[1] Hence there is reason to believe that a major contribution in putting together a strategy for the insurgency came from the Pakistani ISI (see 1.3 *The role of Pakistan*), as well as from Arab fellow jihadists.

The most common description of the post-2001 Taliban insurgency is as a typical case of asymmetric conflict, defined as 'a weaker adversary using unconventional means, stratagems, or niche capabilities to overcome a stronger power'.[2] Undoubtedly, the disparity of strength and resources between the Neo-Taliban and the ISAF/ Coalition was enormous. Given the amount of cash they paid to their fighters and the type and quantity of equipment they used, the Taliban may have spent anywhere between US$25 to 40 million in 2006 to fund the conflict. According to one of Bin Laden's aides, his organisation received US$200 million in financial support from non-state Arab sources during ten years of anti-Soviet jihad.[3] Since some funding is likely to have reached other sources too during those 10 years, it is not unrealistic to estimate that the ongoing insurgency in Afghanistan might have been receiving in excess of US$20 million per year. By contrast the US were spending about US$15–16 million per Talib killed in 2005 and about half that amount in 2006, mainly due to the attempts of the Taliban to fight pitched battles. The monthly US military expenditure in Afghanistan was running at US$1.3 billion in 2006.[4] Thus the tactics and technologies used by the Taliban and the foreign continents are fully consistent with asymmetric warfare (see Chapter 5). This asymmetry is well illustrated in an incident that occurred in Kajaki of Helmand in February 2007: in response to a single round fired by the Taliban, British troops responded with 'dozens of mortar rounds, bursts of red tracers from a 50-calibre machinegun, illumination flares, the flaming rush of a Javelin missile and the juddering explosion of a 1,000kg guided bomb dropped from a Harrier jet'.[5]

However, while asymmetric warfare is certainly part of the Taliban's strategy, it does not cover many aspects of it. Lieutenant General Barno, who commanded the US contingent in Afghanistan in 2003–5, sees Afghanistan as a typical example of Fourth Generation Warfare, borrowing Hammes' development of the asymmetric warfare concept. Fourth Generation Warfare 'uses all available networks—political, economic, social, and military—to convince the enemy's political decision makers that their strategic goals are either unachievable or too costly for the perceived benefit. It is an evolved form of insurgency.'[6] In Barno's words 'Fourth Generation Warfare argues that the enemy's target becomes the political establishment and the policymakers of his adversary, not the adversary's armed forces or tactical formations. The enemy achieves victory by putting intense, unremitting pressure on adversary decision makers, causing them to eventually capitulate, independent of military success or failure on the battlefield.' Barno's is the view from the top, that is the view of a general well aware of the impact of the enemy's strategy on policy makers and public opinions.[7]

passed on information to NATO and government agencies. There were even allegations that the Taliban were willing to offer bounty payments of as much as $250 for the killing of Afghan government officials and civilians working with the foreign contingents. Losses were heavy among district governors and chiefs of police operating in the areas most affected by the insurgency, such as the remote districts of Kandahar, the northern and southern districts of Helmand, most of Zabul and Uruzgan. There were also attempts on the lives of key figures in the region, such as two governors of Helmand, Sher Mohammed Akhundzada and his successor Eng. Daoud. Governor of Paktia Taniwal fell victim to one such attack, while a plot to assassinate Paktia MP Padshah Khan Zadran was also reported. In some cases the insurgents were even reported to have kidnapped relatives of government officials to force them to quit their post or cooperate with the Taliban.[11]

The weakness of the state administration as a key factor in the deligitimisation of government in the eyes of sections of the population has already been identified (see 1.2 *'Rebuilding' the Afghan state*), but the Taliban were quick to target and cause the final collapse of whatever state administration was left. In many districts the threats of the Taliban easily succeeded in driving government officials away to seek refuge in the cities. Most districts in Helmand, Uruzgan and Zabul were either completely abandoned or not functional because of a lack of staff. As early as December 2003 the Taliban were starting to circulate night letters even in the core of the Afghan administrative system in the south, in Kandahar city.[12]

Subnational administrations were not the only form of government presence in the rural areas. In fact, the educational system was in a sense even more important because it was the only service provided by the state at the village level. It is therefore unsurprising that the Taliban immediately started targeting schools. In Kandahar province threats to teachers were already being delivered in late 2002 or early 2003 in some remote areas like Ghorak on the border with Helmand and Uruzgan. Gradually teachers started being threatened in other parts of the province too: Panjwai from October 2005, Dand from May 2006 etc. In other provinces the pattern was similar: threats to the teachers heralded the arrival of the insurgents. In Wardak they started in 2005, in some parts of Logar and Laghman in 2004.[13]

Threats and selective attacks succeeded in closing down schools in many areas (see Table 5). Not only were teachers threatened, but students, schoolgirls and their parents too (see 4.5 *Seeking popular support*). First the insurgents would deliver night letters and oral warnings threatening teachers. and students. In these threats they accused schools of being centres for the propagation of Christianity and Judaism and used changes in the school curricula as a demonstration of the de-Islamisation of the schools. At a second stage, often after many months of repeated threats, actual violence followed. During 2005 and the first half of 2006 at least seventeen teachers and education officials were assassinated throughout Afghanistan, sometimes in gruesome attacks including decapitation. Eighty-five teachers and students were killed during March 2006–March 2007, while 187 schools were attacked. Although the Taliban leadership has denied having ordered attacks on schools and teachers, Taliban militants interviewed by Western journalists have confirmed the use of threats or worse to force schools to close. Moreover, this practice was in line with the rules contained in the Taliban's Layeha, as reported in the press. It is true, however, that, conscious that the villagers often appreciated state education, the Taliban stayed clear of opposing education as such and always declared that what they opposed was mixed male–female classes and the attendance of non-veiled girls, as well as the new curricula and the 'propagandist role' of teachers against the mujahidin. Interestingly, the Taliban did not object to the re-opening of a school in Musa Qala once the British troops had been withdrawn. In January 2007 the Taliban went as far as announcing that they would open their own schools in the areas under their control from March, initially only for boys and later for girls too. The Taliban claimed to be already printing textbooks and to have planned the investment of US$1 million in the opera-

Schools		Total	Open	Closed
Zabul province				
	2006	181		165
Uruzgan province				50
Kandahar				
	2005			49
	2006	335		218
Maaruf district	2004	40		40
Ghorak district	2003	9	3	6
Helmand				
	Jan-06	224	41	183
All south	Nov-06	748		380

Table 5. Impact of the Taliban campaign against schools.

Sources: UN official, Kandahar, January 2006; press reports.

tion. Of course the schools would teach an 'Islamic' curriculum and no maths or sciences would be taught. The announcement suggests that the Taliban must have been considering such a move for some time, given the amount of resources that it would be necessary to mobilise. It is not clear how satisfied parents would be with purely religious curricula in the 'new' schools, but the move might be related to the widespread formation of self-defence units among villagers to protect state schools, which could have affected as many as half of Afghanistan's 9,000 educational institutions.[14]

Doctors too were sometimes targeted by the Taliban. After four doctors were killed in southern Afghanistan, most of those remaining fled the countryside. NGOs, most of which the Taliban viewed as vehicles of moral 'corruption' and as objective allies of international intervention in Afghanistan as well as of the Kabul government, were also extensively targeted (see Graph 3) and not just in southern Afghanistan. In fact, according to an Afghan source, by 2006 the focus of anti-NGO activity had already moved away from southern Afghanistan. In that year the total number of NGO workers killed in the south was just two, if for no other reason than the drastic reduction in NGO activities in the area. By contrast, nine workers were killed in the north, thirteen in the west and four in the Kabul area, although it was not always clear who the attackers

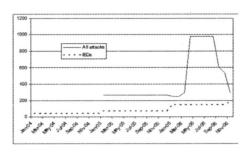

Graph 1. Military attacks carried out by all insurgents in Afghanistan, 2004–6: total and IED attacks.

Sources: press reports, US military, NATO/ISAF.

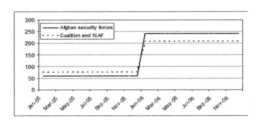

Graph 2. Military attacks carried out by all insurgents in Afghanistan against Afghan security forces and foreign troops.

Sources: press reports, US military, NATO/ISAF.

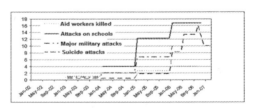

Graph 3. Attacks carried out by all insurgents in Afghanistan: aid workers killed, attacks against schools, major military attacks and suicide bombings.

Sources: press reports, US military, NATO/ISAF.